FOR THE BRIDE COLIN COWIE

FOR THE BRIDE COLIN COWIE

A Guide to Style and Gracious Living

Text by Kathy Passero with Jean T. Barrett

DELACORTE PRESS

Introduction

You're wearing a brand-new, sparkling ring; you had a romantic proposal from your groom; you had a fabulous engagement party; and now you have a wedding to plan. This can and should be the most exciting time of your life.

Over the years I have had the privilege of working with countless brides on their weddings. I always look forward to meeting new brides and grooms and finding out as much as possible about them. I like to know how they met, what they do professionally, where they come from, what ideas they have in mind, what they like and dislike, and where they plan to honeymoon. I always find this enlightening, and it enables me to design a wedding for them that is custom-tailored for their personalities.

Through working with them on their wedding and getting to know them, I have gone on to become close friends with many of my clients. I have been able to watch them in the first months and years of their marriage, as they experience the many changes that married life brings. As I have talked with them about the joys and tribulations of being newlyweds, I have gradually become aware that brides need more than just a wedding planner or picture book; they need guidance on subjects as diverse as entertaining, merging their finances with their husband's, fostering good relations with their in-laws, and keeping passion in the marriage.

I have also made some observations on the brides themselves. Many brides meet me wearing stunning designer outfits, trendy haircuts, the right wristwatch, and killer shoes. When they walk down the aisle, they are absolutely gorgeous and look the epitome of style. Yet in terms of true style–living graciously and treating people with respect and courtesy–some of these brides are sadly lacking. Wedding gifts arrive, and thank-you notes do not follow. Long-standing appointments with wedding vendors are canceled at the last minute. Friends and relatives who perform enormous wedding-related favors, such as hosting a bridal shower or lending their home for the wedding, are never properly thanked and end up feeling slighted.

I don't think that these brides are being deliberately impolite; they are just unaware how important many of life's formalities are. They're not sure how to do things right, and so they decide it's not worth bothering about. They don't have the experience to know that respecting and cultivating the people who are important in your life is one of the most rewarding things you can do.

Today many people believe that style manifests itself in wearing the right designer clothing or perhaps, in the case of brides, registering for the right type of designer items–the ones that magazines suggest are de rigueur for the "stylish bride" this year. To me, style can be interpreted differently; it has nothing to do with how much you spend or what you can and cannot afford to buy. True style is about how we behave and treat one another. It is about living with a sense of self-respect and mutual respect for others.

For better or worse, a wedding is one of those times in life when a bride and groom are very much in the public eye, the center of attention. The bride who knows how to do the right thing in the situations that arise, and makes the effort to treat others with utmost courtesy, is setting the style for her life with her husband. This is a turning point. As a bride, you need to decide whether you want to be known as Mr. and Mrs. Always Late, Mr. and Mrs. Can't Get It Together, or Mr. and Mrs. Forget to Write Thank-You Notes...or if you would rather be respected as Mr. and Mrs. Got It Going On or Mr. and Mrs. Happening!

This is what has motivated me to write this book.

I am sometimes amazed at the change in attitude that happens to brides and grooms after their wedding. During the planning stage and at the wedding itself, the bride and groom are the consummate host and hostess, spending a great deal of time and effort making sure that their guests are pampered, well fed, and entertained. Nothing but the best will do, from the label of the champagne, to the jumbo shrimp at the cocktail reception, to the big-name band, to the vintage Rolls-Royce that speeds them off to their honeymoon hotel. Yet when they return from the honeymoon, they put all their fine wedding china away, lock up the crystal champagne flutes in the sideboard, and settle into a life that revolves around take-out food and evenings in front of the television. So many of the joys of life pass them by.

How much more satisfying it would be to continue the momentum of a wonderful wedding celebration into married life and let the wedding set the mood for life to come. My philosophy for planning a wedding is to fill it with the bride and groom's favorite things–people, food, music, flowers–and make it their own personal statement of style. So wouldn't every bride and groom want to maintain that style in their new life together? By that, I don't mean that you should be opening tins of caviar every evening, or hiring classical violinists to serenade your husband when he returns from work. But there are so many ways to inject style into everyday life and to go the extra mile. On a Friday evening, you can transform an ordinary dinner into a romantic soiree by setting the table with your best china and crystal, dimming the overhead lights, and lighting dozens of candles and placing them around the dining room. On a weeknight, instead of meeting friends at an impersonal bar for a drink, why not invite them into your home for a pitcher of icy Cosmopolitans and some wonderful olives, cheeses, and crusty bread that you picked up on the way home from work? Your friends will appreciate it much more, and it makes for a relaxing start to a great evening.

I am on a mission to help couples fill their lives with style and grace–starting with their weddings, of course, but continuing through their marriages. Planning a wedding provides an opportunity for a couple to establish their personal style and make a statement to their friends and relatives. Every choice made, from the guest list, to the type of ceremony, to the level of formality of the reception and the music for dancing, should reflect the preferences of the bride and groom. When I work with a bride, I always go through a lengthy process to learn her likes and dislikes, in subjects ranging from movies to music, in order to create a celebration that truly expresses her personality and that of her fiancé. At the same time, I make sure that guests at the celebration will be made to feel welcome, cared for, and entertained.

In this book I have provided the same tools that I use to enable you to create a ceremony and reception that will utterly suit you and your groom. I focus not only on flowers, wedding gowns, photography, videography, and wedding cakes but on the importance of behaving with style and grace before, during, and after your wedding.

I think that you will be amazed how a little attention to gracious behavior will enhance your life. When you behave with thoughtfulness and consideration, your efforts will be repaid to you tenfold. Try it. In advance of your wedding, when you and your mother (or sister, or maid/matron of honor) are in the midst of a flurry of preparations, take her out to lunch at her favorite restaurant, and tell her how much her help on the wedding means to you and how much you cherish the time you are enjoying together planning the celebration. When you receive a special wedding gift from a close friend, take the time to write a sincere thank-you note expressing your appreciation for the gift and telling your friend how you plan to use it in your new life.

Planning a wedding that expresses your personal style and that of your groom is wonderful preparation for married life. After all, the wedding is the first fabulous party you and your new husband will host for family and friends. The wedding establishes your style, whether it be casual or formal, country-rustic or city-sophisticated, an intimate celebration for twenty-five friends or a huge bash for three hundred or more. Your wedding registry–the tools you will need in your new life with your husband–should also express your style. I am a firm believer that brides should register for things that they will use, not for items they don't need or are collecting for later–things that will just gather dust in a closet.

In this book I suggest that your wedding can be a springboard for a lifetime of welcoming friends and family into your home and sharing quality time with them. My philosophy of entertaining has always been that the host and hostess should have as much fun as their guests. So many people shy away from entertaining because they think it's too much work or their efforts won't be successful. The icons of entertaining imply that you have to make everything from scratch or do it perfectly. They all missed the point! Entertaining should be easy and all about having fun, not about staying up all night getting the icing on the cake right. We all make mistakes in our personal life and learn from them. Why should the kitchen be any different? I described my approach to entertaining in my first book, *Effortless Elegance*, and I've shared many of my techniques within these pages as well.

Of course, married life is much more than a succession of parties. A healthy marriage takes planning, good communication, and trust. Because advice on how to keep your relationship healthy is even more important than how to choose your wedding flowers, I've devoted a lot of attention to the practical issues of married life: how to merge your finances and plan your financial future; how to settle disagreements; even how to keep sex exciting. After all, most brides spend months planning their weddings; I suggest that equal time be given to planning the important issues that will be the foundation of your marriage.

If you take just one message from this book to heart, I hope it will be that we *can* change the world we live in today and make it a more gracious place. I can't change it alone; nor can you. But together we can make a difference. If we all make an effort to treat each other with a sense of dignity and respect, we'll reap the benefits today and we'll create a brighter, happier, more pleasant future–and a world filled with grace and style.

With my best wishes,

Colin

Chapter 1

Congratulations!

Welcome to the Mr. and Mrs. Club

I t's amazing how one little word–*yes*–can change everything.

Now that you're getting married, not only is your life about to be transformed, but so is your whole attitude. You are no longer thinking for one; now you have another person to consider. From this moment on, for better or for worse, people will think of you as part of a couple. This is one of those rare times in life when you have an opportunity to decide how you will behave toward others and how you want others to perceive you.

Will you be the couple who always arrives late? The couple who never RSVPs but then shows up at the last minute along with an uninvited friend if nothing better turns up? Will you be the people who don't return phone calls, write thank-you letters, or send notes of condolence? Do you want to be known as Mr. and Mrs. Can't Get It Together or Mr. and Mrs. Mess, who never invite anybody over because the house is in a shambles?

I expect you would rather be known as Mr. and Mrs. Got It Going On or Mr. and Mrs. Life of the Party, who are always in the know, throw great informal parties, have the latest CDs, know where to find unusual wines and thoughtful host gifts, and are constantly discovering new restaurants, great theater, and happening clubs.

Of course, you've got a lifetime together for your relationship and your personalities to evolve. But the patterns you set now with your fiancé, family, and friends, as well as the impressions you make at the time of your wedding, often become set for you as a couple in the years to come.

Working Together as a Team

Planning your wedding together is one of the best exercises to help you start thinking as a couple. There are many decisions to be made. You and your fiancé will learn how to negotiate and compromise with everyone from suppliers to attendants, guests, parents, and especially each other. During the months leading up to the wedding, you'll get to better know your fiancé and learn things about him you may never have seen in him before.

Not many years ago, weddings were considered the bride's domain. The groom's role was simply to don a tuxedo, show up, pick up the bar tab, and say "I do" at the right moment. Today, fortunately, all that is evolving. Many grooms are involved in and enthusiastic about their wedding and have opinions on selecting everything from the music to the menu.

When starting to plan your wedding, it is important to sit down as a couple and discuss how you foresee handling the countless decisions you will soon face. If you're not sure how your fiancé feels, ask him for his preferences about the music, for his input on the menu, and whether he wants to help select your china since he will be using it for the rest of his life. I am sure he'll have opinions, and the more his opinions are taken into consideration, the closer your relationship will become. Determine whether you will work together on every detail or whether he will be responsible for some aspects while you handle others. Perhaps he'll choose a lineup of songs and work with the band or deejay, while you discuss decor with your florist.

When it comes to wedding planning, everyone from your mother to your maid of honor may be giving you advice and telling you how things "should be done." While it's wonderful to have help from your friends and family, it is important for you to stay in control of the planning process. After all, this is your wedding and his–not your maid of honor's or your mother's. Be careful to involve your groom in the plans for the wedding as much as he wants to be involved.

Some men say they want no part of wedding planning. If this bothers you, address the issue now. Sit down with your fiancé and explain your feelings. Don't accuse him of being "no help" and don't tell him what he "should" do. Phrase it in a positive way. If it is important to you to have his input, explain to him that he is the most significant part of this event for you, and tell him how much it would mean to you if you planned it together. Add that you are sure he has a lot of wonderful ideas that would contribute to making your wedding special. But bear in mind that while you may be able to coax him into mustering a certain amount of enthusiasm for wedding planning because he loves you, you cannot change anyone's basic personality. If he's just not the type to get involved, don't let this become a major bone of contention.

The good news is that if your fiancé is open to getting involved in the plans and is genuinely enthusiastic about designing a personalized celebration, you have a whole new world of entertaining to discover together.

Doing the Right Thing: *Whose responsibility is it to host an engagement party?*
Traditionally the bride's family hosts an engagement party, but it's fine for the groom's family to be the hosts. A group of friends may throw you an engagement party, or you may host one for yourselves. Engagement parties are by no means mandatory, but an engagement often seems to call for a celebration. If you want to do things a bit differently, almost any get-together can work as an engagement celebration. You don't have to rent the ballroom at the local country club. Instead, why not meet a group of close friends at a favorite restaurant after work for cocktails and dinner? Alternatives include holding a Sunday brunch at your parents' house, or inviting your family and his to an outdoor barbecue in the park. Do what seems most appropriate for you, your groom, and your lifestyle.

Surviving the Emotional Roller Coaster

I have always equated planning a wedding to producing a movie. The difference is, of course, that when it comes to a wedding, you may feel more pressure because you have just one "take" to get it right. It's like live television. Many brides find coping with the stress of wedding planning difficult. Planning a wedding brings up many emotions for those involved. You and your fiancé are not only coping with the stress of planning the biggest party you've ever hosted, but you are also adjusting to a new stage in life and saying good-bye to an old, familiar one.

Likewise, both sets of parents may be facing a tough transition. Sometimes mothers and fathers who seem as if they are being difficult are really just struggling to come to terms with a sense of losing their daughter or son. All these issues need to be dealt with. But don't lose perspective. This is a joyous occasion and a very special time for you and your fiancé. Stay focused on the positive aspects of your engagement and wedding and don't agonize over small details.

Make an effort to keep the fun in your life. Take time for enjoyable activities as a couple. Have a picnic or go for a long hike without discussing the wedding the entire day. Don't let your relationship dissolve into a battlefield over tablecloth colors or tuxedo styles. Keep things in perspective: Remind yourselves that the reason you are getting married is that you love each other and want to spend the rest of your lives together, not that you want to serve duck à l'orange and he wants to serve rack of lamb. Don't let trivial preferences get in the way.

Maintain the same perspective with friends. Your bridesmaids expect to devote time to helping you plan, but that does not mean they put their lives on the back burner for the next six months. When you get together with your bridesmaids, don't just talk about the wedding; make an effort to inquire about what is going on in their lives as well.

Keep a spirit of fun alive in the planning process. Instead of racing out to find a gown and hurriedly checking that item off your list, enjoy yourself trying on all types of bridal dresses to make sure that you have the one you love.

Your wedding day should be filled with memories to cherish forever. Don't waste time worrying about creating the "perfect" wedding. There's no such thing. Weddings are like life; they seldom go according to your finely detailed plan. Often the unexpected event creates the most cherished memory. You need to learn to roll with the punches, have fun, and enjoy yourself no matter what happens.

Understand that for anyone getting married, mixed emotions are normal. A wedding is a joyous occasion, but it can also be stressful. Couples experience everything from sheer bliss to cold feet, from euphoria to sadness and apprehension. Instead of trying to stifle your feelings, find ways to express them, such as keeping a journal or talking with a trusted friend or therapist. Another great way of releasing tension is exercise. Take an aerobics class, or go for a swim, a great run, or a bike ride.

I have a gifted and enlightened friend, Dr. Linda Garbett, a spiritual psychologist who performs many alternative wedding ceremonies. She often reminds brides and grooms that every change in life produces stress. Even if you were to realize you had just won five million dollars in the lottery, your body would register it as a stressful situation by generating a surge of adrenaline. Not to feel any stress during a major life change such as getting married might suggest that you were repressing your feelings or that you were disengaged emotionally from what was happening to you. Linda compares getting married to changing cars in a train–you must always step through a shaky, unsteady section as you move from one car to the next. Recognize it as a natural part of life, hang on, and enjoy the ride. And most of all, learn from the lessons set before you.

It also helps to discuss feelings with your fiancé and your family. If your mother bursts into tears when you announce that you've chosen burgundy instead of the lavender she had picked out, perhaps it's because she feels she's losing you or that her opinions no longer matter. You might want to explain that even though you're getting married, you still love her and plan to stay close. Be aware of her feelings, and make an effort to schedule time with her so that you can reassure her of your love.

Conversely, you often need to assert yourself and to establish your independence from those who still perceive you as a child. This is the time to set the boundaries of your relationships with your fiancé, his family, your family, and close friends. By setting standards from the very beginning, you will earn the respect you deserve and require for a healthy relationship. You can be firm, while still being accommo-dating and gracious. And remember, always be positive, not negative; constructive, not critical.

Welcome to the Family–His, Yours, and Ours

Once engaged, you are taking on a new role within your husband's family. No longer are you just another date; you are part of a larger extended family. As the newcomer, it's important for you to focus on how your behavior can pave the way for long, happy, and healthy relationships. It is not easy to get along with everyone, but you can certainly make every effort to do so, particularly in the early stages of getting to know his family.

There is no better person than your fiancé to coach you on his family dynamics, so discuss your ideas with him before making plans. You wouldn't want to invite his entire family over for a cocktail party to celebrate your engagement only to find out that half the family are teetotalers. Or to plan a steak-and-ribs barbecue for his sister who has been a vegetarian for the past five years.

In order to show your fiancé's family that you genuinely want to get to know them and become a part of their lives, you might take his mom to lunch, go out with his sisters for a cocktail or afternoon tea, or invite his parents over for dinner one evening. These are occasions not to try to impress his family but to get acquainted with one another. Be gracious and be yourself. Remember that the most important thing to your new in-laws is that you love their son. As long as they see how happy you are together, your in-laws should be supportive and accepting.

Your engagement is also an opportunity to set patterns of remembering and acknowledging birthdays, anniversaries, and other special days of family and friends. You're not expected to buy lavish gifts–a nice bottle of champagne, a vase of flowers, a great book, or at least a card will be well received and appreciated. If your fiancé is not current on when these occasions occur, ask his mother or another relative for a list of family birthdays and anniversaries for your own records.

Always be sure to thank your fiancé's family when they host you in their home, make a special effort to help you with wedding planning, or throw your engagement party. A well-written, thoughtful thank-you note shows that you are considerate and caring of those who go out of their way for you.

The same rule applies to anyone who sends you an engagement gift, throws a shower for you, or makes a special effort to acknowledge your engagement. Send a sincere thank-you note and make a phone call to let them know how much you appreciate the gesture. The impression you make now will usually last a long time.

Doing the Right Thing: *What do I do if someone in the family objects to the marriage or if one of our parents refuses to give us their blessings?*

When someone objects to a marriage, it creates a very difficult situation. But if a couple are in love, committed to each other, and have thought through the obstacles to their union, nothing should prevent their wedding. It is up to you, the couple, to behave politely and maturely, no matter how difficult that may be. Explain politely that you hope for your family's support and that you're going ahead with your decision to marry. Continue to handle relations with your family courteously. With time, the detractors may change their minds.

Introducing the Families

Traditionally, the groom's family is supposed to make the first call to the bride's parents. However, if that makes your fiancé's family uncomfortable or if time is simply passing and no one is making an effort to get acquainted, you and your fiancé can arrange for the two families to meet.

When the bride and groom's families have very different backgrounds, it is important to plan the first meeting so that everyone feels comfortable and welcome. Avoid any situation that might embarrass either family. If your fiancé's family is from a small town and has conservative tastes, don't take them to a sushi bar where they might be intimidated by the menu and unable to find anything they like. If backyard barbecues are a tradition in your family but you're unsure whether his would enjoy such an event, ask your fiancé or ask them directly. The most crucial points for both sides of the family to remember are to be courteous to one another and to show mutual respect for you and for your marriage.

A few additional suggestions:

Plan a relatively short event–perhaps Sunday brunch or early-evening cocktails. An all-day drive to a restaurant in the country or other lengthy activities can make people feel trapped for so long that the energy dissipates and they run out of things to say, and they may feel they don't have a way out.

Avoid wedding-planning talk at the first meeting. The mere mention of a catering budget or a ring bearer can sour the conversation faster than politics or religion.

Talk with your fiancé, and note down any common interests you might bring up to get the conversation rolling. Perhaps both families enjoy travel, love wines, collect classical music CDs, or read Tom Clancy books. Ask a few leading questions to break the ice, and show your appreciation of their interests.

Doing the Right Thing: *If we arrange a meeting to introduce our parents, who should pick up the bill?* If you arranged the dinner, then by all means you should pick up the bill. Select a restaurant that is within your budget, and arrange payment with a 20 percent tip included ahead of time by giving your credit card to the maître d'. The way to do this discreetly is to excuse yourself from the table after everyone has ordered their dessert and coffee. Or call in or fax your credit card number a day before to avoid any awkwardness at the table. If your parents or his object, tell them that you would love to let them treat you the next time.

Doing the Right Thing: *How do I arrange to introduce the families if one set of parents is divorced? By bringing them all together or by planning separate events?* If the divorced parents get along well and feel comfortable together, invite them together. If, on the other hand, they don't get along, arrange for separate introductions. If one lives far away, it is not essential to arrange a prewedding meeting.

Chapter 2

Making Your Statement of Style

Planning the Wedding

Weddings are changing. The average wedding is certainly smaller than in the past. The bride and groom are more involved in the planning, and the mothers are less involved. There are more interracial, intercultural, and interfaith weddings than ever before. All this has paved the way for us to create wonderful new rituals and trends. We've broken the barriers of the etiquette-ruled, can-and-cannot-do wedding. Now it's time to be inspired and to do things that are indicative of who you are.

More and more, the couples I work with are receptive to new ideas when it comes to planning their wedding. Outdated traditions are finally falling by the wayside. Brides and grooms have the freedom to design weddings that express their personal style. Couples often write their own vows. Some couples incorporate poetry, readings, and songs into their ceremonies; others mix various religious traditions such as the Jewish breaking of the glass with Buddhist chants and Indian cuisine for dinner. There is much more use of color in the decor, and the bride is no longer restricted to wearing a full, long, white dress. Likewise, the groom does not have to look like a penguin in a rented tux. Some brides are rejecting the standard grouping of bridesmaids and groomsmen in favor of having only children as attendants. Others are opting for no bridal party at all. At the reception many couples are cutting the garter toss and the receiving line out of the program entirely. Instead of one formal affair, weddings are becoming three-day destination celebrations that combine relaxed and casual events with more elegant, formal ones.

One of the most practical new trends is the wedding website. When my friends Gary and Marla Wolfson got married recently, they invited many guests from Canada, Hong Kong, London, South Africa, and other parts of the world. Since people were traveling such a long distance, the couple scheduled events over a period of four days. To keep their guests informed about all aspects of the wedding–from the logistics of driving to the synagogue and booking hotel accommodations to providing information about the bridal party–they designed a wedding website. For Gary, who specializes in Internet development professionally, creating an online dimension was a natural addition to his wedding and a practical, cost-effective way to communicate with family and guests. Of course, it's not necessary that you create a wedding website, but you can send wedding-related information to your bridal party, friends, and other guests via e-mail and keep your online friends up to date.

Content for a Wedding Website

- Date, time, and place for ceremony and reception
- Directions
- Parking information
- Suggestions for attire (black tie, cocktail attire, casual, and the like)
- Miniprogram for the weekend or for the wedding day
- List of nearby hotels (include prices, rates, descriptions, and maps, as well as toll-free phone numbers and fax numbers; if you've booked a block of rooms for a discounted rate, note what name and rate the guests should ask for). If your hotels have their own websites, consider providing links on your page.
- Information on airlines offering reduced fares to your destination and links to the airlines' websites
- Information about the town where you will be getting married, along with suggestions of activities for out-of-town guests, including good restaurants, museums, walking trails, and so on. Here too, if the city or certain attractions in town maintain their own websites, you might want to provide a link on your page.
- Pictures of yourselves as children and teenagers
- A short story of how you met, how he proposed, and the like

(For Gary's many relatives who live far away and had never met Marla before the wedding, these last two items were particularly helpful. Both the pictures and the story gave them a chance to learn about Marla and to feel as if they were getting to know her.)

Creating the Big Picture

Whenever I plan a wedding with a couple, I interview the bride and groom at length as a way to begin defining their sense of style. As a designer, I need to know all I can about their likes and dislikes. I'm interested in their favorite colors, flowers, foods, hobbies, movies, art, cities, and vacation destinations. It is equally important to me to learn what they dislike. This helps us begin to draw a mental picture of the wedding they want.

It is just as important for you to do this in order to paint a detailed verbal picture to all the vendors who are going to be part of your wedding design and planning process. You and your fiancé will want it clearly understood who you are, what you like, what you don't like, and what you are prepared to spend, so that you will be able to create a wedding that is entirely yours.

Following is the list of questions I ask my clients. Look it over, and answer the questions with your fiancé. Your answers should provide insight on the style of celebration that is right for you.

1. What are your favorite restaurants? Describe why you like them–the atmosphere, type of cuisine, quality of food, the way the food is served, and perhaps the way the restaurant is decorated. If there is an element that your favorite restaurants have in common, what is it? What is it about your favorite restaurants that you might wish to incorporate into a great wedding reception?

2. What are your favorite foods? Are there types of foods–French, northern Italian, Indian, Japanese, Southwestern barbecue–that you love? What are your least favorite foods? Are there certain dishes from favorite restaurants that you

love, such as a grilled vegetable salad, or the way a local bistro prepares duck breast? This information will help you better direct your caterer.

3. What sort of food service do you prefer? Is a formal sit-down dinner your idea of an ideal party? Do you enjoy cocktail parties and tray-passed foods? Or do you prefer a buffet, where you can pick and choose? Do you enjoy dining casually or more formally?

4. What are your favorite drinks? Do you prefer wine, beer, spirits, or soft drinks? Do you have a favorite cocktail? Does your fiancé love micro-brews or single malt scotch?

5. Where do you like to spend your vacation? What appeals to you about this destination, and why? Is it formal or relaxed? Cosmopolitan or rustic? On the beach or in the country?

6. What are your favorite books or stories? What sort of atmosphere does your favorite book or story create? Are there ways to incorporate elements of this into a wedding celebration?

7. What is your favorite film, and why do you like it? Are there scenes from a favorite movie that really speak to you? Do you remember wedding scenes that you love from films, such as the nuptials in *Four Weddings and a Funeral* or *Father of the Bride*?

8. What is your favorite flower? Are there flowers you dislike? If you don't know the specific names of flowers, think about what colors and types of flowers appeal to you. Look through books and magazines, and note or clip photos of the ones you like and dislike.

9. What are your favorite and least favorite colors? Consider how your favorite colors translate to

• Pictures and miniprofiles of your attendants and relatives, to help guests know who's who

• A list of stores where you're registered and links to the stores' websites

• A paragraph about and/or picture of where you're going for your honeymoon

• Anything else you think might be fun and helpful for your guests

Focus on providing helpful information rather than including elaborate graphics that will take a long time to download, especially for those whose computers may be slower than yours.

different types of fabrics that might be used in wedding attire or decor. You may even find samples in your wardrobe or around your home.

10. Does a particular time of day or season of the year inspire you? Do you love sunsets? Do you love the cozy feeling of being indoors after a winter snowfall? Do you love long summer evenings outdoors? How might you translate this to your wedding?

11. Do you have a favorite collection that might offer a theme for your wedding? Perhaps you collect majolica pottery, vintage linens, or crystal decanters. Incorporating a collection of beautiful things that have meaning to you is a lovely way to personalize a wedding celebration.

12. Do you have a hobby or pursuit that you want to incorporate into your wedding in some way? If a couple loves to sail, a seaside wedding at a marina or yacht club or even on a rented boat might be appropriate. If you love opera, perhaps your celebration should include some of your favorite arias performed by a local opera singer. If you enjoy collecting wine, then fine wine might become an integral part of your celebration.

13. What clothing designers are your favorites? What specifically about their designs appeals to you? Is it the lines of the clothing, the use of color, the fabrics? Is there a fabric you are particularly fond of, a trim you have always admired, a silhouette you love?

14. Do you have a fairy-tale image of being a bride from your childhood? Do you have a childhood wedding fantasy? Or a contemporary one?

15. Do you see your wedding as a single event, or would you like to have a series of events over several days, such as a weekend-long celebration?

16. What is your favorite type of music? Make a list of your favorite composers and their works, or artists and their songs. Be sure to also add a list of songs that you definitely do *not* want to hear at your wedding!

17. What are your favorite photographic styles? Do you like black and white, color, or sepia? Do you like a photojournalistic, documentary, or traditional portrait approach?

18. When you can do absolutely anything, or nothing at all, how do you spend the day? Would you love to spend a day pampering yourself at a salon, or would you prefer a great hike in the mountains? How could you translate that to your wedding day? What special magic is there in that choice?

Based on your answers to these questions, you may identify a unifying theme–a thread of style that you can weave through your wedding. Your theme might relate to a favorite movie, a color, a poem, or a favorite flower, but it should be something you love, such as gilded antique picture frames or the lush look of an overgrown Irish garden. Whatever it is, your theme should help you create a consistent style for your wedding that is evident in everything your guests encounter, from the invitations, to the menu, to the cake, to the band that plays for dancing after dinner.

Be Prepared

Before meeting with your vendors, determine what you are prepared to spend, and make a detailed list of what you like and what you don't like. Supplement this by collecting as many magazines as you can and creating two piles of clips: one for ideas you like and another for those you dislike. Don't limit yourself to bridal books. A picture of a beautiful room in a decorating magazine might trigger ideas for your reception setting. Or you might come across an unusual shade of celery green or pale peach that you want to incorporate into your attire or decor. Use a clear plastic file to hold clippings, and keep notes handy to show suppliers. Many brides also find it useful to carry a notebook or tape recorder to jot down or record wedding-related thoughts and ideas as they occur. Doing your homework in advance will give your vendors the direction they need, and it eliminates many potential problems by creating a visual presentation to back up your discussions.

When it comes to describing what you want for your wedding, a picture is worth a thousand words. Someone I know learned this the hard way the morning of her wedding. She had described the bouquet she wanted to her florist–an unstructured cascade of hydrangea, ivy, and roses in muted pinks and tea shades to match the fabric flowers on her gown. The florist glanced at a picture of the gown, took a few notes, and assured my friend she knew exactly what she wanted. The wedding morning arrived, and so did the bouquet–cotton-candy pink roses and baby-blue hydrangea fashioned into a very tight nosegay. "It looked like a Easter bonnet," my friend remembered. "It clashed horribly with my gown and the setting, both of which were subdued and romantic."

Fortunately, the florist was present and eager to please the bride, and she created another bouquet at the last minute. But this story illustrates that what *you* think you're describing precisely can often generate a totally different mental image to someone else. Had my friend given her florist a picture of the flowers and look she liked, or possibly a photo of the exact bouquet, I am sure that her problem could have been avoided.

Wedding Professionals–What They Bring to the Picture

When you are ill, you visit the doctor. When you build a house, you work with an architect. So when you decide to get married, I urge you to hire a wedding planner. A professional wedding planner has worked on dozens if not hundreds of weddings and is capable of anticipating and preventing a myriad of problems that a less experienced person might not be able to foresee. A good planner is also able to assemble the right team of skilled professionals, from caterer to photographer, to ensure your wedding is the event you dream it will be.

If your budget won't allow you to enlist the services of a professional, your caterer or banquet director may be able to assume this responsibility. Or you might want to plan the wedding yourselves and hire a consultant for a few days before your wedding and for the wedding day itself to make sure things run smoothly and according to plan. Another possibility is to ask a friend or family member with good organizational skills to take care of organizing all the details so that you can relax on your wedding day.

Be careful when selecting the person you will be working with on your wedding. Just as you don't look in the Yellow Pages for a doctor or architect, do your homework when seeking a wedding consultant. Ask a trusted friend whose wedding you attended and enjoyed very much, or ask your florist or caterer if they could recommend someone. Planning a wedding is a very intimate experience. It's essential to find a person you get along with and who makes you feel comfortable. After all, you're going to be spending a lot of time together, and you want to make sure that your taste and the consultant's are similar. If not, you could be in for a difficult time rather than an enjoyable experience.

Make sure from the beginning that he or she understands exactly what you want, what you don't want, and what your budget permits. Find out his or her fees; some planners charge by the hour or by the day; others charge a flat fee per project or a percent of the total budget. Ask about markups for the food, flowers, service, and other items. Find out whether the bridal consultant is receiving a commission from any suppliers and, if so, how much. Consultants are entitled to make a commission as long as they disclose it to you since you are footing the bill. But, you won't want to be pushed into working with certain florists, caterers, or photographers just because they're giving a commission to your consultant. You'll want to work with vendors who share your sensitivities and taste. Find out who will be signing the contracts for each of the vendors, as well as how and when payments must be made. Ask to see portfolios of the consultants' work, and obtain references from former clients–then call them to check that they were satisfied. It's also a good idea to ask the consultants to describe their worst disaster and how it was solved.

Finally, confirm that the consultant is actually going to be at your wedding–not just sending a junior staff member–and that he or she will be there for the duration of the festivities and not leave right after the ceremony.

About Money

Traditionally, paying for the wedding was the responsibility of the bride's parents. But today, depending on the financial resources of the people involved, couples do everything from paying all expenses themselves to splitting them between their respective families.

I've always believed that style has nothing to do with spending large sums of money. In fact, some of the most tasteful weddings I've attended were simply and inexpensively done. It would be foolish to put yourselves–or your parents–into debt for the next ten years just to throw the most extravagant wedding in town.

If you haven't planned a wedding before, chances are you will be surprised at how quickly all the costs add up. Brace yourself for a long list of expenses, many of which you might never have considered, such as postage for invitations, officiants' fees, equipment rental, marriage licenses, maître d' tips, and so on. Oh yes, and don't forget the honeymoon costs if they're part of your budget!

To develop your budget, complete these steps:

1. Take the time to discuss with your fiancé (and your family, if applicable) who is going to pay for which expenses.

2. Come up with a ballpark figure of what you can spend on the entire wedding.

3. Make a list of as many items as possible that you will need to account for in your budget. Among the items to remember:

• Ceremony costs (site, music, officiant, marriage license)

• Reception costs (site, food, beverages, service, bar, entertainment, decorations and lighting, gratuities)

• Attire (bridal gown, shoes, lingerie, jewelry, hair, makeup; gowns, shoes, hair, jewelry, makeup for bridesmaids). Traditionally, the bride and/or her family covers these expenses. But attendants frequently pay for their own attire these days. If that's the case, keep their financial resources in mind when you select their attire.

• Jewelry (wedding bands and engraving)

• Invitations, place cards, host cards, thank-you notes. Include postage. Remember, you'll need to put stamps on all your response envelopes.

• Ketubah for Jewish ceremonies

• Flowers (centerpieces; altar flowers; bridal bouquet; tossing bouquet; attendants' bouquets; boutonnieres for groom, groomsmen, and fathers; corsages for mothers and grandmothers; other decorative flowers such as wreaths, and pomander

Elegance on a Budget

If you are on a limited budget, here are some time-tested ways you might consider to keep wedding costs down.

• Instead of skimping on ten items, splurge on five. Make a list of everything you want at your wedding, figure out what's most important to you, and toss out the rest. Instead of having a formally seated dinner reception with a live band and dance floor, opt for a chic and elegant cocktail party with a groovy jazz trio and tasty hors d'oeuvres.

• Keep the guest list small, and have a small bridal party.

• There's no law that invitations must be engraved or professionally printed. If you have artistic talent, design and print them yourself, perhaps combining an unusual computer font with distinctive handmade textured paper that you've found in a specialty stationery store or art supply shop.

• When shopping for wedding attire, don't limit yourself to bridal salons. A great alternative is to shop at local department stores or even vintage clothing shops until you find an off-the-rack dress you love, then add special touches like a chiffon or velvet wrap, a veil, jewelry, or gloves. You'll create a more personal look.

• Check local fabric shops for unusual fabrics to overlay as tablecloths. A seventy-two-inch square is enough for a sixty-inch round table. If you have a favorite color, juxtapose it with complementary shades. Layering lavender chiffon over dark purple damask and pale green over dark green silk is much more striking than draping everything in the same color.

• For a country setting, you can create place cards by writing or painting guests' names on pieces of fruit, such as pears or apples, which can also be spray-painted gold or silver for an antiqued look.

• If you're on a budget, avoid big "wedding" bands. They tend to be pricey and play old standards your guests will have heard at twenty other weddings. Consider a smaller, more unusual group based on your musical tastes (like a swing or R&B combo). Or make several hours' worth of mixed tapes of your favorite songs, and ask a music-loving friend to act as your deejay in lieu of giving a traditional present.

• To save on the cost of champagne, serve champagne cocktails using a domestic sparkling wine with peach juice to make Bellinis, orange juice to make mimosas, or cassis to make kir royales. Or serve a cocktail du jour, such as a tray of Manhattans or whiskey sours instead of champagne at the reception.

• Ask a close friend or relative with good organizational skills to act as a wedding-day problem solver if your budget doesn't allow for a professional coordinator. Working off your schedule of events (we'll talk about this later on), have your friend call each vendor the week before the wedding to answer questions and explain last-minute changes. Discuss your concerns, so he/she will feel comfortable making decisions on your behalf. If you don't do this, everyone from the caterer to the cook will head to the one person they recognize–the woman in the wedding dress–whenever a crisis arises.

balls for the ceremony and reception; ladies' room bouquet)
• Gifts for attendants, ring bearers, flower children, parents, and for each other
• Photographer and videographer
• Transportation
• Rehearsal dinner (traditionally paid for by the groom's parents)
• Honeymoon
• Accommodations (wedding night) or rooms for out-of-town guests if you are paying for them. Today most guests who travel to a wedding pay for their own transportation and accommodations.

A Word to the Wise

When negotiating, always look at the whole package. If a vendor comes up with a preliminary budget that exceeds your limitations, attempting to break the costs down bit by bit to shave seven dollars here or five dollars there will only alienate the vendor and frustrate you. There's nothing wrong with negotiating; it's all in how you do it. It is much more gracious to explain that the estimate is more than you can spend. Then ask the vendor to offer suggestions on how to reduce the cost. Vendors will often come up with creative solutions you would never have considered, and working together you will be able to trim the budget without cutting back on the items that are most important to you. Perhaps you'll serve only three appetizers rather than six at the cocktail hour. Maybe your family and friends are not interested in wine and would be perfectly happy with a snappy cocktail, such as a martini, a gimlet, or a mint julep.

If the vendor's estimate comes in slightly higher than the limit you specified, be gracious and explain that you have to stick within your budget. But if you have clearly communicated your budget limitations to the vendor and he or she has presented an estimate that exceeds your budget significantly, you should ask yourself: Why is this vendor being so unresponsive to my directions? Is this really the person I should be dealing with?

Finally, don't expect discounts, even if you have a friend in the wedding industry. People often think that because they know someone who works for a hotel or a caterer, they are automatically entitled to receive major discounts or free services. The fact is that if a hotelier, caterer, or florist friend wants to give you a discount, they will offer to do so. If they do not offer you a discount, chances are they are either not authorized to cut prices or are unable to do so for other reasons. If you are working with a friend on your wedding and he or she does not offer you a discount, *do not ask for one*. You will only put your friend on the spot by bringing up the subject, creating an awkward situation for both of you.

Chapter 3

Bridal Registry

Selecting Items That Suit Your Lifestyle

One of the first things you are likely to do as you begin to plan your wedding is to register for the items you will need to set up your new home with your husband. It's a good idea to do this sooner rather than later if you want to avoid being deluged with boxes full of gifts chosen by everyone except yourself. But I can't stress enough how important it is to choose items you'll use and that reflect your lifestyle. Think about the way you live. Is it casual? Do you live in a small apartment with little storage space and where you can better accommodate a buffet than a sit-down dinner with friends? Do you have a garden with an outdoor barbecue area where you grill dinner every night in the summer? Do you invite friends over often? Do you plan on entertaining a lot, and if so, do you cook? If not, don't register for crates of formal dinnerware and crystal that you'll end up stowing away to collect dust. Instead, register for things that reflect your lifestyle now. Later in life, as your taste level and your income develop, there will be plenty of time to collect more fine china. *The primary reason to register is so that you have the tools for starting your life together, not to put things in the closet for later use.*

Some couples are very outdoorsy and register for items like grills and backpacks. Others love games and might register for a special chess

Typical Bridal Registry

To help you start thinking about your wedding registry, the following is a checklist of the major categories and items that many couples need. Each retailer has its own system for registration. All major stores are fully computerized, and some allow you to scan in items electronically as you walk around. Remember that you are by no means obligated to register for any item simply because it's "traditional." Choose what fits your lifestyle, whether it's china, home exercise equipment, or a beautiful wicker picnic basket.

Fine China/Formal Dinnerware

Dinner plates, salad plates, dessert plates, bread and butter plates, cups (coffee, tea), saucers, chargers, mugs, soup bowls, cereal bowls, creamer, sugar bowl, coffeepot, teapot, gravy boat, salt and pepper shakers, serving bowl(s), serving platter(s), soup tureen, candlesticks, demitasse or espresso cups

Casual/Everyday Dinnerware

Dinner plates, salad plates, dessert plates, bread and butter plates, cups (coffee, tea), saucers, mugs, soup bowls, cereal bowls, creamer, sugar bowl, coffeepot, teapot, salt and pepper shakers, serving bowl(s), serving platter(s), candlesticks, demitasse or espresso cups

Fine Crystal

Water goblets, white wine glasses, red wine glasses, all-purpose glasses, champagne flutes, cordials, highball glasses, brandy snifters, sherry glasses, liqueur glasses, beer mugs, pilsner glasses, fruit juice glasses, iced beverage glasses, old-fashioned glasses, ice bucket, decanter(s)

Everyday Glassware

Water goblets, white wine glasses, red wine glasses, all-purpose glasses, beer mugs, pilsner glasses, fruit juice glasses, iced beverage glasses

Silver Plate or Sterling Flatware

Dinner forks, salad forks, dessert forks, dinner knives, soup spoons, tea spoons, iced tea spoons, cocktail forks, serving pieces, butter spreader, serving spoon(s), serving fork(s), gravy ladle, pasta server, cake knife, pie server, serving set, hostess set, chest to hold flatware

Casual/Stainless Steel

Dinner forks, salad forks, dessert forks, dinner knives, soup spoons, tea spoons, iced tea spoons, serving spoon(s), serving fork(s), gravy ladle, pasta server, cake knife, serving set

Cookware

Casserole dish, lasagna pan, soufflé dish, roasting pan, skillet, saucepan(s), omelet pan, steamer, griddle, double boiler, thermometer, trivet, cutting board, cheese board, mixing bowls, measuring set, cake pan, cookie sheet, muffin tin, knives, knife block, steak knives, punchbowl/glasses, corkscrew, bar tools, teakettle, canister set, spices, spice rack, measuring spoons

Appliances

Coffeemaker, espresso/cappuccino maker, coffee grinder, toaster/toaster oven, microwave, mixer, can opener, juicer, steamer, rice cooker, food processor, blender, water filter, slow cooker, bread machine

Miscellaneous

Candlesticks, napkin rings, coasters, wine rack, hot pads, oven mitts

Table Linens

Formal: tablecloth(s), napkins, placemats, runner(s)

Casual: tablecloth(s), napkins, placemats

or backgammon set. Perhaps your grandmother plans to give you a set of vintage china as a wedding gift. In that case you might want to focus on casual china as well as other items for the kitchen, such as a food processor, a knife set and block, or an espresso machine. Remember, the bridal registry is *not* limited to tabletop items. You might want to register for good-quality sheets and towels or even furniture. You might also consider registering at more than one store to create variety or to add to an existing collection. Browse through magazines, and take a few afternoons to shop with your fiancé and talk honestly about what you both need and will use.

I always recommend owning one basic set of good china, crystal, and silver. This gives you a solid foundation from which to build. Just as you own a quality suit and change its look with accessories such as belts, scarves, and shoes, you can accessorize your table. From the base of a good set of china, you can mix and match items for a creative, eclectic look. You might choose a five-piece place setting in a particular pattern and augment it with sets of bowls, salad plates, or serving pieces in a complementary color and pattern, possibly even from several different manufacturers.

Most of us give a lot of thought to our personal appearance. Your clothing tells people who you are and makes a strong personal impression. Your table can also provide people with a window into your lifestyle. It should reflect your personality and allow you to continually reinvent it by using different colors of napkins, centerpiece containers, or sets of vintage plates or flea-market finds. Just as you would never limit yourself to a monochromatic wardrobe in one fabric or style, don't limit your table.

I get many questions on how a bride is supposed to let her friends, relatives, and wedding guests know where she is registered. Let me state unequivocally that *a bride should never volunteer registry information without being directly asked; nor should registry information appear on printed materials relating to the wedding*. The way friends and relations find out where you are registered is to ask your mother, your maid of honor, or you. If guests want to know, they will ask. There is no way to tastefully give out registry information. Printing registry information on an insert in a wedding invitation looks like exactly what it is: a blatant solicitation for gifts. I do make a slight exception in today's high-tech world; if you have a wedding website, I think it's fine to include "Wedding Gifts" as one page, where you can list the names of stores where you are registered and, if available, provide links to the stores' websites. Guests who choose to access that information can click on the link, making gift shopping quick and easy.

Bed Linens

Sheet sets, flat sheets, fitted sheets, pillowcases, pillow shams, bedspread, comforter, dust ruffle, duvet, duvet cover, blankets, mattress pad, pillow protectors

Bath Linens

Bath towels, hand towels, fingertip towels, washcloths, bath sheets, bath rug(s), shower curtain, shower rings, tub mats

Luggage

Suitcase, carry-on bag, garment bag

For the Home

Vacuum cleaner, iron, ironing board, toolbox, tools, grill, hope chest, clock, lamp(s), mirror(s), rug(s), curtains, television, VCR, camera, camcorder

A Dinnerware Primer

Porcelain: Favored for its strength and translucence when held up to light; smooth texture; generally designed in off-white or ivory. Formal.

Bone china: Made from the same materials as porcelain along with animal bone ash; favored for its warm luminescence; less translucent than porcelain. Formal.

Earthenware or pottery: Heavy, porous, and opaque; made from baked clay fired at a low temperature; less durable than stoneware, but known for its rich clarity and variety of colors and patterns. Casual.

Stoneware: The most durable type of pottery; opaque, nonporous, and clay-covered; fired at a high temperature to create the hardness of stone; possesses a glossy finish that is microwave and dishwasher safe. Casual.

Adapted from *Inspirations: The Bloomingdale's Home Planner*

A Glassware Primer

Lead crystal: Fine glass with a lead content, which makes the glass clearer.

Colored glass: Mineral salts, such as copper to create the color green, are melted with glass to render specific colors.

Cut glass: Designs are cut into the base, stem, and sides of the glass by hand or machine.

Milk glass: A tin oxide and sometimes a tint are added to create an opaque, milky effect.

Etched glass: The glass is coated with wax with certain areas left as a design and then dipped into acid to fix the design on the glass; usually reserved for fine crystal.

Engraved glass: Delicate designs are cut lightly into the glass, generally by hand; usually reserved for fine crystal.

Pressed glass: Raised designs are formed in the glass before it cools, creating a three-dimensional pattern.

Adapted from *Inspirations: The Bloomingdale's Home Planner*

A Flatware Primer

Sterling silver: Sterling silver flatware is made from silver that is at least 92.5 percent pure. With proper care, sterling flatware should last for a lifetime or more. It may be put in the dishwasher. Sterling and silver plated flatware both have to be polished from time to time.

Silver plate: Silver plated flatware can be an economical choice with much of the beauty of sterling. It is usually made of nickel or brass with a thin coating of pure silver. Plated flatware can become scratched; if so, it can be replated. It is usually dishwasher safe.

Stainless steel: Durable and relatively inexpensive, stainless is a practical choice for an everyday set because it will not tarnish, chip, or wear out. It is dishwasher safe.

Vermeil or gold electroplate: This gold-colored flatware is manufactured using a thin layer of gold (usually of 10 karats or better in quality) applied to metal. Gold over silver is called vermeil; gold over another metal is referred to as gold electroplate.

Chapter 4

People Politics

Balancing What You Want to Do with What Everyone Else Is Telling You to Do

You've just announced that you're getting married, and already there is trouble in paradise. Your mother calls to tell you she's checked with your family minister, priest, or rabbi, and his calendar is clear. Your future mother-in-law wants you to meet her for lunch at her country club which she *just knows* would be ideal for your reception. Your roommate is clipping out pictures of bridesmaids' dresses she likes–and you haven't even asked her to be your bridesmaid yet!

Most engaged couples get too much advice and input from well-meaning moms, relatives, and friends. I run into this myself all the time with brides and grooms. Even though my clients and I have discussed their vision for their wedding, a maid of honor or a mother pulls me aside and spends ten minutes explaining how it was done at her wedding. "It worked so beautifully! Wouldn't it be just perfect for my daughter, too?!"

Now is the ideal time to start setting boundaries and establishing your independence. Wedding planning is a great opportunity for you and your fiancé to stand up for yourselves and establish your taste and style as a couple. Whether you plan a traditional wedding with a religious ceremony and a large, sit-down dinner-dance reception, or an alternative approach to your nuptials, this is *your* wedding and you need to make your own decisions.

Keep in mind that friends and relatives who offer suggestions are really only trying to help, and you should deal with them kindly. In some cases they may be a source of great ideas. But if their suggestion is off-base, let them down gently. Say, "You know, that's a nice idea, but it doesn't really fit what Brian and I have planned." Then explain your approach, and be sure to thank them for their suggestion. Chances are the friend or relative will immediately understand that you have your own well-thought-out ideas about your wedding, and they will respect you for it.

Who's Who in Your Bridal Party

Tempting as it might be to discuss your wedding at length with every friend while you are in the early stages of planning, use discretion in discussing your bridal party. Never casually ask someone to be in your wedding party. First, sit down with your fiancé and decide how large a bridal party you want, whom you want to include, and whether you want to have an equal number of men and women. Keep your friends' personalities in mind; supportive, low-maintenance friends and family members invariably make the best bridesmaids and groomsmen.

When considering bridesmaids and particularly maids of honor, ask yourself how this friend or relative has behaved in the past when you have sought out her help. Was she responsible and eager to be of service to a friend in need? Was she selfish and resentful? Well intentioned but slightly scatterbrained? Does she have a new boyfriend whom she'll be draping herself over at your wedding when you need her help most? Does she have small children whom she will have to look after during your wedding ceremony? Is she likely to drink a bit too much and forget things? Also, ask yourself whether you could be creating any potential time bombs by including friends in your bridal party who used to date or had a falling out.

Another point to consider: Has your friend been asked to serve as a bridesmaid four times in the past year? If so, she may be a little burned out. Or she may be suffering from the always-a-bridesmaid-never-a-bride syndrome. In that case you might well make her feel worse by asking her to join the bridal party than by simply inviting her as a guest. If you are unsure as to her feelings, let her know you would like for her to be involved but will understand should she wish to come simply as a guest.

When you ask someone to be an attendant, let them know what you want them to do. If each bridesmaid will be assigned a specific task, put it in writing for her. One person might be responsible for making sure the guest book is signed. Another might collect disposable cameras from the tables at the end of the evening. A third might help the photographer locate specific family members or friends to be photographed. (You should provide a list of these people for the photographer and bridesmaid.)

Keep your friends' finances in mind, too. If a friend is watching her budget very carefully, you could put her in an awkward situation by asking her to spring for a $200 gown, $150 shoes, plus the cost of helping to throw a shower and bachelorette party in addition to the shower and wedding gifts she is already planning to buy for you, and the cost of an air ticket and hotel room.

There's no obligation to have a large wedding party; many brides opt for no attendants, or they choose just a maid or matron of honor or a single attendant. Another option is to showcase as many children as possible. They always bring "oohs" and "ahhs" when they're part of the bridal party. The entire bridal party can be composed of children, or they can simply be part of the entourage. Just keep in mind that kids are not small adults. Many children, particularly very young kids, can become shy or frightened at a wedding with so many strangers around. If you want young children to play a role in your wedding, take care to rehearse them well so that they are comfortable with everything they have to do. Be sure they are well rested, fed, and taken to the bathroom before the ceremony.

Bribes are not entirely out of the question, either. One of my favorite ways to convince stagestruck children to walk down the aisle is to tell them there's a gift for them if they make it through the ceremony or that one of the groomsmen has candy in his pocket. As soon as the ceremony ends, present them with a doll, toy, stuffed animal, or a small basket of candy or cookies.

Many brides have lots of close friends but want only a small bridal party. This needn't be a problem. There are other ways to honor friends without asking them to be bridesmaids. If one of your friends has a beautiful voice, you might ask her to sing a song during the ceremony. If you have a close friend whom you think might be hurt not to be included in your wedding party, take the time to explain that you are only having your sister as matron of honor, or that you are limiting the attendants to your two cousins–whatever your rationale is.

Doing the Right Thing: *What should I do if I have already selected my bridesmaids, but my future sister-in-law seems to assume that she will be a part of the bridal party?*

There are many ways to single out a family member or close female friend aside from asking her to be a bridesmaid. You might consider asking her to do a reading during the ceremony, to make a special toast, or to take part in the wedding in some other capacity if you'd rather not include her as a bridesmaid. Today many brides decide that, rather than include the traditional bridal party in their wedding celebration, they will invite friends to participate in another way. For example, actress Lisa Kudrow has a wide circle of friends, but she didn't want to have twenty attendants. Instead, she walked down the aisle accompanied by her mother and father. Prior to the ceremony, ten of her close friends each walked up to Lisa and presented a flower, which her mother tied with a large ribbon, making a beautiful bouquet that symbolized her close ties to the important people in her life.

Chapter 5

Designing a Personal Ceremony

The ritual that unites you and your fiancé is arguably the most significant part of your wedding day. Yet until recently it was the one aspect of the wedding where the bride and groom had little input or even no control at all. The couple would spend months personalizing everything else, only to leave their actual union in the hands of their parents, pastor or a complete stranger.

Today, more and more couples are stepping outside traditional constraints and designing unique services that reflect who they are and what they believe. Some couples recite Shakespeare sonnets or original poetry that they've written to reflect their feelings for each other. Others pay homage to their family's traditions by mixing elements of their religions.

Because the ceremony is so important, you should sit down with your fiancé and discuss your preferences early on. If both of you are from the same religious and social background, you may easily agree on a traditional ceremony. But that situation occurs less and less frequently. Today there are more interracial, interfaith, and intercultural marriages than ever before. Ceremonies that reflect this diversity can be very meaningful.

Overall, there are four major types of ceremonies:

• Religious: Imbued with the beliefs and rituals of faith, the ceremony is performed by a priest, minister, rabbi, or other ordained official.

• Interfaith: When individuals of different faiths are joined in marriage, the ceremony may be performed by two officiants, one from each faith, or by one officiant who is familiar with both religions.

• Secular or civil: In a civil service a judge officiates, using a nonsectarian text.

• Spiritual: Increasingly popular, spiritual ceremonies emphasize humanistic values rather than a religious belief system.

In considering what type of ceremony will be best for your wedding, think over your spiritual values and traditions, and those of your fiancé. What are your goals for the ceremony? What personal standards, ethics, and codes do you live by? How do you see yourselves in the world? What religions do your families practice? What do you want to include from those religions? What are your visions for the family you're going to create? What traditions do you want to incorporate into the ceremony?

If you would like other individuals or families to participate in the ceremony, who are they and how would you like them to play a role in your ritual? Are there children who might take part as well?

Remember that you are in charge of your ceremony. Even if you are opting for a traditional religious service, you should understand and approve every element of the ritual. You don't want any surprises when you and your groom are standing in front of two hundred friends and family!

When you meet with your officiant, come armed with your ideas and input for the ceremony. Ask lots of questions so that you can begin to shape the ceremony that is right for you. Many officiants like to personalize the ceremony by sharing details about the bridal couple, so you should provide information on how you met, your courtship, your plans for the future, and so on. Other couples prefer to have the officiant stick to the traditional text, without sharing private details of their lives. Whatever your preference, be sure to communicate it clearly to your officiant.

Here are some questions to keep in mind when you meet with your officiant. Ask the rabbi, priest, minister, or whoever else is officiating about his or her plans for your ceremony:

What kind of ceremony do you give?

What do you want to know about us?

What will you be saying about us?

How are you going to present us?

How long will the ceremony last?

If your ceremony will include information about you and your groom, make a list of significant points about yourselves and your relationship to help the officiant get to know you.

Where and how did you meet?

What attracted you to each other?

Why did you fall in love?

How long have you been together?

Why did you decide to get married?

What does marriage mean to you?

What do you respect and love most about him/her?

What zany and odd quirks does he/she have that you adore?

If an officiant seems unreceptive to your comments and questions or reluctant to stray from his standard service to personalize one for you, perhaps you should look elsewhere. Otherwise you may end up with a dry, canned service that has little meaning or significance to you and your fiancé.

Many of the ceremonies I have witnessed in recent years have incorporated nontraditional symbolic and spiritual elements that are meaningful to the couple and to the congregation. Here are some ideas from spiritual psychologist Dr. Linda Garbett to consider adapting for your ceremony:

• Place four poles around the altar where the couple will stand–similar to the *chuppah* of the Jewish ceremony, but not necessarily with a canopy. As your guests arrive at the ceremony, have someone give each of them a long ribbon and ask them to write out a message on it. The message can be a word, a wish, a phrase, a line of poetry, or anything else they think is appropriate. Prior to the ceremony, have the guests walk up and tie their ribbons around the poles, embracing the bridal couple with their good wishes and blessings. Or you might include the ribbon in the invitation or welcome package at a "destination wedding." Add a note explaining the ritual that will take place during the ceremony and your desire to have them be a part of it.

• Create an ancestor tree–a small topiary with pictures of beloved family members who have passed away. These can either be pinned to the topiary or put in small decorative frames and hung from its branches. Place the tree on the altar or near the entrance to remind you and all your guests of your lineage and of the fact that your wedding will add a new chapter to your family's history. You can create this same concept using a decorative arch or a pole.

• For a nighttime wedding, have all the guests hold candles, then have the bride and groom light a unity candle, then light the maid of honor's and best man's candles. The maid of honor and best man then light candles for the other bridesmaids and groomsmen and pass the flame on until every guest has a lit taper. This bathes the ceremony in a romantic light. At the end of the ceremony, the candles can be placed in a box of sand near the exit.

• Another dramatic option for an evening wedding is for each guest to hold a lit candle in a small candleholder. Before the end of the ceremony, the officiant asks the guests to pass the candles to the person seated at the aisle who places them along the edge of the aisle. This creates a brightly lit path encompassing all the spiritual energy of the guests for the bride and groom's recessional.

• For a spiritual outdoor wedding or Native American theme, incorporate the four elements of earth, air, fire, and water. To symbolize earth, place to the north a decorative bowl containing a small amount of earth from a place that is significant to you as a couple. For air, place incense in the east. For fire, place a candle in the west. And for water, place a bowl of water in the south. You can choose to light the candle and incense beforehand or incorporate lighting them into your ceremony. (The items symbolizing the four elements may either be placed in various corners of the room or arranged on small pedestals around the altar.)

• A couple who believes in astrology might incorporate this belief system into their ceremony. One way to do this is to fill two small decorative bowls with petals from the flowers that correspond to your astrological signs. During the ceremony the officiant transfers both sets of petals into one larger bowl, blends them, and sprinkles the petals over the bride and groom as a symbol of their unity.

Unless you are being married in a strict religious ceremony, it is acceptable to borrow elements from ceremonies that appeal to you. I like the Quaker tradition, where there is no third-party officiant to pronounce the couple married. Instead, the couple themselves decide to marry each other and ask each guest to sign the contract as witnesses. Today some couples have an artist or calligrapher design a modernized version of the Quaker marriage contract with lovely scrollwork and illustrations– similar to a Jewish *ketubah*. It creates not only a treasured keepsake to frame but a record of all the names of those who shared in your celebration.

Chapter 6

Who, Where, When, and Why: Details on the Guest List, Location, and Timing

Guest List

As a first step in determining the invitation list for your wedding, sit down with your fiancé and discuss what size wedding you envision. Determine whether you prefer an intimate affair with only your nearest and dearest friends, or whether you adore huge parties where every coworker and distant relative is going to be included. It's helpful to write down a list of the people you definitely want to invite and those whom you might include if you opt for a larger celebration. Many elements of the celebration will depend on who is paying for what, what size wedding you prefer, and how many guests you and your fiancé have already put on the list. Don't forget to give each set of parents a certain number of guests to invite.

When it comes to wedding guest lists, the general rule of thumb says to figure that only 80 percent of those invited will attend. However, don't count on it. Always make sure that the site you choose could accommodate every guest you've invited in the event that *everyone* is able to attend. It's also a good idea to be able to accommodate a few extras in case you inadvertently failed to invite someone important to you.

Given your budget and the number of guests you would ideally like to include, ask yourselves what type of wedding will work best for you. If your budget is somewhat limited and you're committed to inviting 250 guests, a sit-down dinner with dancing may be too costly an approach. Bear in mind that it is always better to do a few things well than to try to stretch your budget to cover a lot of things scantily. Rather than scrimp on dinner for 250, consider timing your wedding to take place in the early evening and hosting an elegant cocktail party with a variety of tasty hors d'oeuvres and food stations. Or consider an afternoon tea with a selection of finger sandwiches, a beautiful wedding cake, and a chamber music quartet–or your favorite music recordings.

If, on the other hand, including an elegant sit-down dinner is high on your list of priorities, perhaps you and your fiancé should consider reducing the guest list. The same is true if you have your heart set on being married in your own home or in a charming courtyard attached to a historic town house, either of which might accommodate only fifty guests comfortably. You could limit the wedding to an intimate group of close friends and family members and then host a large cocktail party or backyard barbecue when you return from your honeymoon.

If you are fortunate enough to have unlimited resources, you might need to make only a few compromises to balance your budget, your guest list, and your vision for your wedding. However, I

There's No Place Like Home

Special considerations apply when a friend or family member has offered you the use of their home, either for a pre- or postwedding party, or perhaps for the celebration itself. It is a lovely and generous gesture for someone to loan you a home for your wedding festivities, and for the bride and groom, it is a responsibility that should not be taken lightly. Many relationships have soured over the fact that someone loaned a home for a wedding or special event and the party-giver failed to handle the situation properly.

First of all, recognize that you are in someone's home, not a hotel or restaurant. Be sure you and your wedding vendors understand which areas of the house are off-limits to wedding workers and guests. Everyone working in the house should be briefed on the fact that it is a private home and special care must be taken to avoid damaging the house and its furnishings. You should also discuss with the owner whether a special insurance rider may need to be taken out to cover your event, which would be your financial responsibility.

As your schedule of events is finalized and delivery times are set, a complete schedule listing all vendor arrival and delivery times should be given to the homeowner so that he or she knows what to expect.

always remind brides that wedding planning is like marriage itself. It is all about learning to negotiate, compromise, and invent creative new strategies to find a happy medium that will please you both. It's good practice for a successful marriage.

Doing the Right Thing: *Is it acceptable to invite single friends without a guest?*

Weddings are not singles' bars or parties; instead, the guest list is composed of the people who are nearest and dearest to the bride, the groom, and their families. It is socially acceptable to invite single guests without pairing them with a date. However, use your best judgment in this situation. If a friend of yours is in a serious relationship, it is considerate to invite the friend and his or her date. If space or budget limitations absolutely prohibit this, it is a good idea to call your single friends and explain the situation. That way they are less likely to be offended or to assume that you are slighting their relationship. If you do invite friends and their guest, take the time to call and get the correct spelling of the guest's name. It is not very pleasant to arrive at a wedding and find that your place card reads "Guest of Mr. Smith."

Selecting a Location

The questions you answered in the preceding chapters about your tastes and preferences hopefully have sparked a few ideas and visions for the type of setting you want to use as a backdrop for your wedding. Be creative and think beyond the basic country clubs and hotel ballrooms. Perhaps a friend of yours is willing to offer a charming beach house as a site for a ceremony and tented reception. If you and your fiancé are both confirmed oenophiles who met at a wine-tasting, a vineyard or winery wedding might be ideal for you. If you both adore weekends in the country, you might choose a rustic barn with a view of rolling hillsides. Sophisticated urbanites might opt for a private room at a top restaurant or a penthouse loft with a nighttime view of the city.

You might also do what more and more couples are doing—hold different events spanning an entire weekend. This approach often includes a rehearsal dinner on the Friday evening, the wedding itself on the Saturday, and a farewell brunch on the Sunday. If this takes place in a town in which neither of you live, it is referred to as a destination wedding. When planning a destination wedding, keep in mind the distance factor as well as the cost of accommodations at the location you wish to select. Choose a destination that will be within the budget of your guests so that a maximum number will be able to attend.

Think also about the time of day and the season you prefer. So many couples want to marry in May, June, or September, which puts a lot of pressure on the top wedding sites and vendors. If you decide to hold your wedding during the "off-season," such as early spring or midwinter, chances are you will have better access to the best locations and suppliers. Of course, certain locations have a definite seasonality factor, which can work with you or against you. I love the idea of holding a reception at a ski resort during the summer, when the meadows are carpeted with wildflowers and the rates are lowest. However, if

On the day before or morning of your event, have a beautiful floral arrangement or other personal gift, along with a sincerely written thank-you note, delivered to the homeowner. Be sure that throughout your function, there are workers assigned to handle cleanup and to take care of any spills or other problems. After your event is over, the house should be professionally cleaned and all trash and other evidence of your party removed from the property. It's not enough to merely fill a dozen black plastic trash bags and leave them for the poor homeowner! When you leave, there should be no sign that your party ever occurred. Be sure to have a worker on standby to remove any broken or damaged items and to replace them or have them repaired on the first business day after your event.

And after your wedding, take a moment from your honeymoon to personally call your friend or relative and thank them for the loan of their home. A written thank-you note should be sent as a follow-up, underscoring how much it meant to you to use their beautiful home for such a special occasion in your life.

you envision an outdoor wedding by the shore in Maine, you'll want to limit yourself to July or August.

Time of day is another major consideration. A midmorning wedding followed by a wedding breakfast or lunch is an offbeat and charming approach. Likewise, an outdoor wedding held at dusk, taking advantage of the changes in light caused by the setting sun, has a wonderful aura of mystery. When you decide on the time of day for your wedding, be sure to visit your venue at that same hour so that you can check how the light is falling and where the best locations are for photography.

Holding your ceremony and reception in the same spot simplifies matters. However, if you have always dreamed of a reception at home and a ceremony in the church or synagogue you attended as a child, by all means incorporate both locales into your celebration. If possible, limit the driving distance between the two to twenty minutes or less. If this is not feasible, consider providing transportation for guests between the ceremony and reception in the form of buses, vans, limousines, or Town Cars.

One caveat: Inquire about the site's rules and restrictions in terms of food service, decor, music, parking, and so on before you sign a contract. You wouldn't want to hire a ten-piece band to perform at a reception site that has stringent noise restrictions. Don't assume that the site will be yours to do whatever you like on your wedding day without written confirmation as to when and what hour the room will be made available to you, what you are allowed to do in terms of decorating and lighting, the time by which you will need to vacate, and so on.

It's also important to inquire as to whether there will be another wedding on site the same day yours will take place. It's best to have the venue on an exclusive basis. However, if this is not possible, make sure all logistics are well orchestrated to avoid confusion among your guests, band members, florist, and other suppliers and to ensure that no one arrives at the wrong celebration.

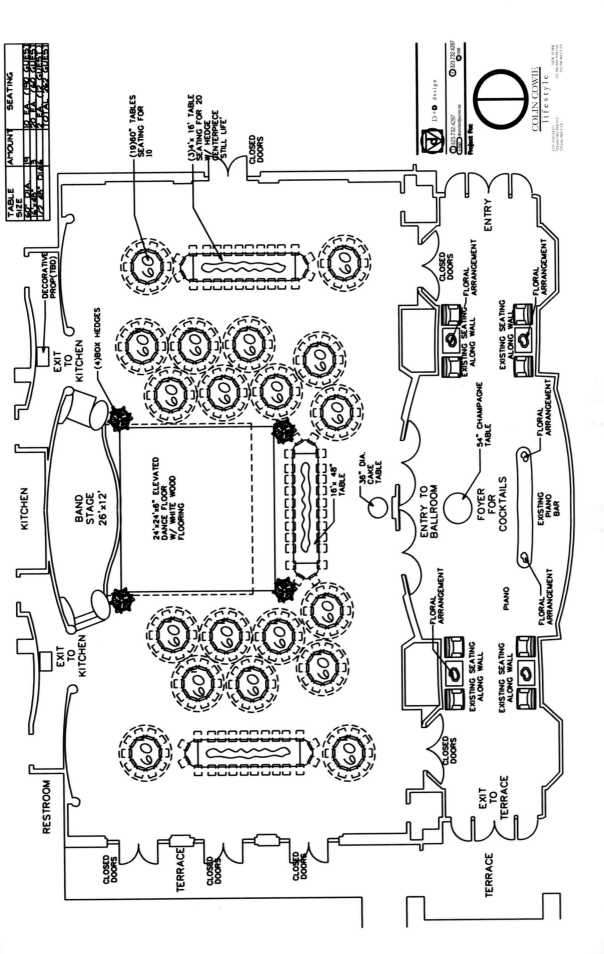

TOGETHER WITH THEIR FAMILIES
JENNY McCARTHY
AND
JOHN ASHER
INVITE YOU TO CELEBRATE
THEIR MARRIAGE
SATURDAY, THE ELEVENTH OF SEPTEMBER
NINETEEN HUNDRED AND NINETY-NINE
AT SEVEN O'CLOCK

SAN YSIDRO RANCH
900 SAN YSIDRO LANE

The pleasure of your company is requested
at the rehearsal dinner for
Jennifer and Nicholas
on Friday, the thirty-first of July
at half after

Please arrive
March 11 – March 14 1999

Chapter 7

Pulling It All Together: From A to Z and Back Again

Invitations and Calligraphy

After you've chosen the date, location, style, and level of formality of your wedding, the next step is to create your invitation. Invitations can often take a month or more to write, design, and print, so work on a typical invitation usually begins at least three months before the wedding date.

Once there was only one correct format for wedding invitations. They were engraved on white or ecru card stock with black ink and worded according to a strict set of rules. Today we take a less structured approach and have much more opportunity to express ourselves creatively. Many couples design their own invitations using an unusual textured or colored paper, an elegant computer font, and adornments such as sealing wax with a stamp of their initials or a ribbon in the wedding color. Another possibility is to contract with a designer or artist to create a one-of-a-kind invitation. Even a traditional invitation can be enhanced by wrapping it in soft tissue or parchment paper and tying it with a beautiful ribbon as a finishing flourish.

The tone and style of your invitations should reflect the tone and style you have selected for your wedding, whether it's a formal black-tie evening or an elegant afternoon tea. An invitation with flower petals blended into the actual paper stock or a flower pressed inside would be charming for a garden wedding. For bride Vanessa Angel we wove an angel motif throughout every detail of her celebration, from the table decorations of gilded cherubs holding ivy, hydrangeas, and roses, to the invitations embossed with a tiny antique gold angel.

Think through what information needs to be provided to guests in addition to the basic invitation to the ceremony and reception, and a response card and envelope. Many invitations now include practical information such as driving directions to the ceremony and reception, parking instructions, and other necessary details. If you're planning a weekend-long celebration, the invitation is a convenient place to extend an invitation to a farewell brunch the morning after the wedding, a rehearsal dinner the night before, or whatever other events you wish your guests to attend. By planning ahead and working with a good stationer or designer, all the elements can be designed to work together as an attractive package rather than a miscellaneous collection of cards and envelopes.

Note that while a wedding invitation can and should include practical information on the details of your celebration, as I've said before, the invitation should never include information on where you've registered for gifts. Wedding guests who are interested in sending you an appropriate gift will check with you or your family directly or visit your wedding website.

Once you've received a layout of the invitation, proofread it *very* carefully and ask your fiancé, your mother, or a friend to proof it, too. Double-check dates, addresses, phone numbers, and times. This is one situation where one typo can spell disaster. Don't forget to print a return address on the envelope so that if one of your guests has moved, you will find out earlier rather than later.

Envelopes may be addressed by hand in neat script or done in calligraphy, whichever you prefer. The stationery store from which you obtained your invitations is usually a good source for calligraphers. There are many styles of calligraphy, so always ask for a sample of the calligrapher's work. Other printed components relating to your wedding, including host cards, place cards, table numbers, and menus, may also be done in calligraphy to match your invitations.

One more caveat: Be sure to weigh an invitation at the post office with all the enclosures to make sure you have the correct postage.

Composing the Invitation: Who, What, Where, When

There are many traditions about invitation wording, and you should feel free to follow them closely or disregard them entirely if you like. If you are having a formal church wedding, you will probably want traditional, formal wording in your invitation. If you are holding a small wedding at home, perhaps a handwritten letter-style invitation is more appropriate. Entire books have been written on the subject of how to compose a wedding invitation, so it's impossible to completely cover the subject in the space of just a few paragraphs. Here are a few guidelines, however.

At its most basic, an invitation tells you *who* is doing the inviting; *what* the event is; *where* it will be held; and *when* it will be held. The wording of your invitation will depend to a large extent on *who* is issuing it and *where* the event or events will be held. Traditionally the bride's parents issue the wedding invitations, but a bride and groom can also issue their own invitations, or a groom's parents may issue the invitations. Keep in mind that the purpose of the invitation is not to signal who is actually *paying* for the wedding. For example, if the groom is financially well off and is paying for the entire celebration, the invitations would generally still come either from the bridal couple or from one or both sets of parents.

Weddings at a house of worship traditionally are worded to "request the honour [or honor] of your presence." If the ceremony is to be held at another location, the invitation line generally reads "request the pleasure of your company."

There are well-established traditions for wording invitations from parents who have divorced. Each spouse is mentioned on a separate line, with no *and* between the lines. Generally, if one or both of the parents have remarried, only the original parents' names are mentioned, although if there is a particularly close relationship between the stepparent and the bride or groom, it would be appropriate to include the new spouse's name.

It's a good idea to familiarize yourself with the traditional modes of wording a wedding invitation. Then you can make an informed decision whether to follow those traditions. If you are completely in the dark about how wedding invitations are traditionally worded, you may make a mistake that can confuse or even offend relatives or other guests.

Invitation Timeline

Order invitations: 3 to 4 months in advance

Mail save-the-date cards: Up to 6 months in advance

Mail invitations: 6 to 8 weeks in advance

Mail rehearsal dinner invitations (if separate): 3 to 4 weeks in advance

Mail postwedding brunch invitations (if separate): 3 to 4 weeks in advance

Working with Color

There are no rules when choosing colors. Your wedding is an opportunity to create a visual statement of style, to paint a picture to your family and friends of who you are, and to create a window into your soul. If you love green, use it abundantly. If the calligrapher tells you that you must use black ink, find a new calligrapher.

When selecting colors, try to create a multidimensional scheme. For example, if you adore the color lavender, give it more emphasis by layering lavender chiffon over deep violet, mint green, and chartreuse, creating contrast and impact. I urge you to do the same with whatever colors you choose. Be open and think creatively. Mix and match swatches of fabric to explore complementary colors. Perhaps you'll discover a combination that had never occurred to you. Don't be afraid of rich, full hues. If you love deep burgundy, sable, or even papaya, by all means use them generously.

Layering contrasting colors works even with the lighter, more traditional bridal shades. Add colors like mushroom, champagne, parchment, taupe, flesh, and various ivories to white for visual interest. In fact, I rarely work with stark white unless I am making a very contemporary statement, as it tends to look one-dimensional, and it is difficult for most brides to wear a stark white dress. Softer ivories and eggshells are warmer colors that look much more flattering in photographs against flesh tones. The same holds true with colors on video: The camera tends to slide over stark white, leaving viewers with no sense of dimension, whereas layers of color add depth and visual interest.

Flowers

Flowers are a universal language that every bride understands. As you begin to explore what types of floral decor to use, keep in mind the prevailing tone and style of your wedding. Centerpieces of wildflowers and aromatic herbs placed in a variety of antique pitchers fit a rustic, country-garden wedding. A more formal affair might call for dramatic baroque topiaries. If you've selected chic simple sheaths for the bridesmaids to wear, choose chic understated bouquets to complement them.

To begin the process of deciding on your wedding flowers, browse through bridal, home, and garden magazines and clip photos of flowers and arrangements you like and dislike. Also, talk to friends whose weddings you thought were beautiful for personal recommendations of florists. It is a good idea to interview several florists in order to find one who responds creatively to your ideas and preferences. Once you have found a florist you like, ask for references from other recent brides, and call them. When talking to former clients, find out if they found the florist punctual, reliable, and professional, and whether the florist delivered what was promised. There is nothing worse than walking through the church doors to find the florist sweeping out the back door and nervous energy filling the air. Also, confirm that the florist you have met with (not an assistant) will do the installation at your wedding.

Help your florist by providing him or her with a photo of your wedding dress, and arrange for the florist to visit the ceremony and reception sites with you to discuss ideas. Creative florists can offer an array of decorative options beyond flowers, including candles (or electric candles if the site prohibits real ones), various types of lighting, topiaries, aisle runners, arches, wreaths, swags, ficus trees, trellises, potted palms, and other decorative items.

A good floral designer will also come up with new alternatives to consider. For an autumn wedding, we scrapped the traditional aisle decorations of expensive flowers and instead collected huge garbage bags of fallen leaves in rich shades of yellow and brown. We used the leaves in abundance to make a tapestry of fall foliage ankle-deep around the ceremony area and up and down the aisle. You might do the same with flower petals for a spring or summer wedding.

When Kenny G married Lyndie Benson, we layered mismatched 1950s tablecloths on every table. For centerpieces we used silver coffeepots, creamers, and sugar bowls filled with fragrant rosemary, thyme, lavender, and cabbage roses for a country-garden ambience. The effect was beautiful, and after the wedding Kenny and Lyndie retained the vintage pieces to enhance their home's decor and to use again and again when entertaining.

Flea markets are a great source for vintage linens and antique silver teapots, candlesticks, and other items to mix and match on the tables at your wedding. Vintage items are not only affordable but add texture, color, character, and variety to your tables.

Doing the Right Thing: *What if my friends want me to toss my bouquet, but I want to preserve it as a keepsake?*
Ask your florist to create a smaller "tossing bouquet" that resembles your bridal bouquet. The tossing bouquet should be placed on the cake table to enable you to find it easily. Many florists automatically

include a tossing bouquet in the budget, but never assume.

Although the bridesmaids and groomsmen needn't have flowers that replicate yours, they should complement your bridal bouquet style (bold and contemporary, French country, and so on) and color scheme (pastels, jewel tones, and the like). One lovely look is to create tightly packed nosegays of roses with a slightly different shade for each bridesmaid. Nosegays in the same color but using a different flower for each are also pretty. Consider adding a touch that reflects the ambience of the location, such as shells at the beach or berries, acorns, and oak leaves for a fall wedding.

Instant Glamour

At the reception, the first impression created at the entrance, as guests arrive, is one of the most important visual effects you can create at a wedding. It's wise to invest a little more on a beautiful swag across the entrance or a garland lining the stairway leading to your reception.

One of the best ways to set a mood is with lighting. For Don Henley's outdoor wedding to Sharon Summerall, we created a romantic effect by arranging hundreds of candles in the grass surrounding the altar and ceremony area. You can transform an indoor setting the same way by placing votives or candles on tables, on every ledge, and in every corner. Candles are less expensive than pinpoint spotlights and twice as romantic. Most manufacturers offer a discount if you order them in bulk.

For evening weddings, you can add romance

Bridal Bouquets

Arm bouquet: A bouquet that is held loosely in one arm

Cascade: As the name suggests, a bouquet that spills forward to create the effect of a waterfall of flowers

Hand-tied bouquet: A bouquet that is fastened together with a ribbon rather than tightly wired

Nosegay: A round upright bouquet of flowers clustered together tightly, generally with the stems in a holder supplied with a small amount of water to keep them fresh

Pomander: A tightly constructed bouquet, usually shaped like a ball or heart, and covered on all sides with blossoms; usually carried on a ribbon around the wrist; also frequently hung above an altar or doorway

Teardrop: A tight cascade bouquet in the shape of a teardrop

Wired: A bouquet where the stem of every flower is individually wired into a certain shape, such as a heart, a circle, or even a pocketbook

Hints for the Budget-Conscious Bride

• Instead of large, costly floral centerpieces, fill a decorative urn with green grapes and apples or red grapes and pomegranates, surrounded by greenery and studded with a few full-blown roses. It looks impressive, and it costs a fraction of a traditional floral centerpiece.

• Large bowls of brightly colored, richly textured fruit like lemons and oranges or even sugared fruits make impressive, inexpensive centerpieces.

• Low baskets or terra-cotta planters filled with flowering plants and herbs are another option.

• Use inexpensive, attractive groupings of three small antique silver vases packed tightly with flowers alongside three or four tall silver candlesticks or a picture in a silver frame. You will use fewer flowers while creating a rich, abundant look.

• Instead of an elaborate arch of flowers, hang a wreath studded with flowers and adorned with candles and ribbons above your heads at the altar.

and drama with dim ambient lighting and pinpoint spotlights on the centerpieces and other focal points. When planning your lighting, find out whether the site has dimmer switches on the lights. If not, consider adding dimmers for your event if the site will permit it; dimmers are not that expensive to buy and install, and the results are well worth it. Under no circumstances should you use florescent light. It cannot be dimmed and is very unflattering. Understand that what is lighted will draw the eye, and anything in darkness will disappear.

To Everything There Is a Season

Keep seasonality in mind when selecting the flowers to use in your bouquets and at your reception. While florists can now access blooms imported from all over the world, choosing seasonal flowers may be far less costly. Some types of flowers are available virtually year-round, while others are more seasonal and may be expensive if you order them out of season. Your florist is the best source of information on what is available at the time of your wedding, but here are some rough guidelines on floral seasonality:

Generally Available Year-Round Baby's breath, cornflower, delphinium, gardenia, Easter lily, lily of the valley, orchid, rose, snapdragon, stephanotis

Available in Spring Apple blossom, calla lily, daffodil, dogwood, forget-me-not, forsythia, freesia, geranium, iris, jasmine, jonquil, larkspur, lilac, narcissus, peony, sweet pea, tulip, violet

Available in Summer Aster, bachelor button, calla lily, cosmos, iris, larkspur, Queen Anne's lace, sweet pea, tuberose, zinnia

Alexander von Sandenberg

In honor of
___y and Michael Donahue
Menu
___ushroom Ravioli in Veal Sauce
___rispy Porcini Mushrooms and
___ Fresh Tomatoes with Chives

___let Mignon with Bordelaise Sauce
___ on a nest of Crispy Leeks
___ Roasted Fingerling Potatoes
___ Medley of Green Vegetables

___f Watercress and Endive
___ Balsamic Vinaigrette

___Dessert Medley
___ Cake Raspberry Sorbet
___ Petit Fours
___ Tea and Cookies

February 14, 2003

Available in Winter Acacia, calla lily, camellia, forget-me-not, holly, iris, sweet pea, tulip

Available in Fall Aster, dahlia, shasta daisy, tuberose, zinnia

Innovative, Delicious Menu Ideas for Your Wedding and Afterward–at Home

Just as creative new approaches are surfacing in wedding ceremonies and attire, creative new flourishes are appearing on the menu. Wedding receptions no longer require an enormous sit-down dinner or even a traditional buffet. An elegant wedding breakfast with tangerine mimosas (sparkling wine and tangerine juice), caviar or crab omelettes, and fresh peaches for dessert is a great way to entertain your guests. Or consider a summer garden luncheon under a tent with delicious chopped barbecued vegetable salad and grilled leg of lamb.

Another trend is exotic appetizers to add panache, from sushi for a couple planning a honeymoon in Japan to something as quirky as frankfurters for a couple who met at a World Series game. Not only will an original menu with a twist present a refreshing surprise to your guests, it will add a much more personalized touch to your wedding than would serving the expected overdone roast beef and chicken à la something.

In designing the menu for your wedding, the first thing you'll want to do is to establish the capabilities of the caterer or hotel. Begin by looking over the caterer's or hotel's menus to give you a sense of the type and style of food that they usually serve. You will get the best results by staying within the capabilities and experience of the food-service provider, not by asking for an overly elaborate menu that they will have difficulty executing for your guests. Remember that it is easy for a caterer to prepare a delicious sample menu for two people, but when it comes to translating the same menu into a meal for one hundred or two hundred wedding guests, it might not work–especially if your celebration will take place outdoors or in another locale where extensive kitchen facilities may not be available.

If you are ever in doubt, opt for simplicity. You can make a statement of style with one or two spectacular dishes. For example, instead of having ten different tray-passed appetizers during the cocktail hour, serve mountains of jumbo shrimp or sliced smoked salmon. I would rather enjoy a simple, freshly prepared dinner any day than fancy food–something that's been stuffed, flambéed, and gratinéed, with a sauce on the side. I always opt for quality produce and do as little as possible to it.

Balance the menu by avoiding repetition of any of the ingredients. Alternate hot and cold courses (perhaps soup followed by a salad followed by a hot entrée, for example), and always select a first course that is not only spectacular in presentation but also can be served either ten minutes early or twenty minutes late, depending on how the timing of the day is going. The first course is very important because people are hungriest and will remember it best. Food is life theater. What happens in the first five minutes sets your mind for the rest of the show. Start with a colorful, three-dimensional dish with an interesting combination of textures and tastes, such as a salad with grilled prawns, or a colorful vegetable terrine with a red pepper coulis.

Always ask for an advance tasting of your menu, which should be scheduled for a couple of weeks before the wedding date. The tasting allows you to see how the menu looks and tastes and to make any changes that you feel are necessary. Scheduling the tasting to occur shortly before your wedding date will help ensure that your changes will remain fresh in the mind of the caterer or chef.

Ideally, schedule the tasting in conjunction with the florist, so that a table can be set with the linens, candles, place cards, glassware, and a sample centerpiece that will be used for the wedding. Make sure the florist is on hand to discuss any changes you might require. I recommend photographing the sample centerpiece to document it, and counting specifically how many flowers are used. If there are twenty white roses, thirty gardenias, and fifteen sprays of lily of the valley, document it and keep this as your record. Florists often use more blossoms for a trial run in the hope of impressing you.

While you should expect to pay for the sample centerpiece, the tasting meal for two should be gratis if you have already retained the services of a caterer. You should offer to pay for any additional guests you arrange to bring along.

Your tasting meal is an important form of insurance. It gives you the opportunity to make changes and ensure that you get precisely what you want. And believe me, it's easier to make changes a week or two before the wedding than when a hundred appetizers are plated and ready to be sent out to the tables.

Just Desserts: The Wedding Cake

One of the most enjoyable parts of planning a wedding is creating your wedding cake, the crowning glory of your celebration. No longer is the only choice a filigreed, swagged, beflowered, multitiered extravaganza topped by plastic bride-and-groom figurines. Cake specialists have become culinary artists, offering an imaginative palette of colors and flavors. Your cake might be a sleek, elegant confection sheathed in rolled fondant; an asymmetrical tiered whimsy reminiscent of the Mad Hatter's hat in *Alice in Wonderland*; or a delicate Wedgwood-blue cake that mirrors the colors of the wedding.

Because the best bakers book up well in advance, you will want to retain a baker several months ahead of your wedding date. I recommend choosing a baker who is willing to create a unique cake for you, one that reflects the style of your wedding. Thus, I always leave the cake until last to design, after the attire, decor, and menu of the wedding have been determined.

When you begin to work with a cake baker, take with you a photograph of your dress, a swatch of the tablecloth you plan to use, and a few photographs of the site where the wedding reception will take place. Let the baker know whether it will be a black-tie or casual affair, whether it will be daytime or evening, and so on. Look through the baker's portfolio to choose a basic style or technique of a cake, whether it be round, stacked, square, or perhaps a combination, such as a square base with round rows at the top.

When it comes to personalizing your cake, the possibilities are almost limitless. I have taken the pattern on a tablecloth and used the same pattern in icing all over the cake. Another time I focused on a particular flower attached to the bride's dress and had that flower appliquéd all over the cake. For actress Holly Robinson's wedding to Rodney Peete, for which the reception took place on a tennis court, I designed a latticework around the sides of the cake that echoed their garden theme. For Hugh Hefner's wedding, for which we stitched up and scalloped the tablecloths, we created the same effect for the cake with a swag designed in icing all the way around the top.

When finalizing your menus and head count, remember that it is your responsibility to make sure that all the suppliers who will be providing services at your wedding are fed. This includes band members, photographers, videographers, the wait staff, and so on. It isn't necessary to provide an entire meal or to set a table for them; you can arrange for a simple buffet with an assortment of salads and soft drinks or grilled chicken and pasta set up in a back room somewhere on site. You can even arrange to have a deli tray delivered with soft drinks. Whatever you decide, these people will be working very hard for you, and *everyone* works better on a full stomach.

Photographers: Their Style Versus Yours

Wedding photography has become much more creative over the last decade. In addition to the traditional posed portraits, many couples now opt for a journalistic approach that will capture that special unexpected moment when the best man's toast brings tears to the groom's eye, or the behind-the-scenes images of a bride securing her father's boutonniere on his lapel minutes before their walk down the aisle.

Although the trend in the 1970s and 1980s was toward exclusively color photos for weddings, black-and-white has made a definite artistic comeback. Many couples now opt for a combination of black-and-white and color photographs, while others create a nostalgic look with sepia prints, or hand-painted or hand-tinted photos, in which the bride's bouquet might be in color while the rest of the photo is black-and-white.

When selecting a photographer, look through as many samples of his or her work as possible. Bear in mind that any portfolio submitted for you to review is a collection of the person's very best photos. It might be the fifty best shots out of thousands taken over a career. Look not only at the images but at the quality. Are the colors rich and vibrant? Are the images in focus and well framed? If you're planning an outdoor wedding, does the person's outdoor work look clear and make good use of natural light? Does the photographer seem to understand how to work with both natural and artificial lighting? If you're planning a wedding in a wine cellar or church with low lighting, how adept does the person seem to be at working in those conditions? Does the photographer understand composition, how to organize and frame the elements in a shot to best advantage?

If you choose to work with a photojournalist but also want traditional portrait-style shots, make sure the photographer you choose works with a medium-format camera as well as a 35-millimeter. A 35-millimeter camera produces pictures with a grainy look that works well for candids but not for portraits.

In addition to discussing the photographs, talk with the photographer about whether he or she is bringing an assistant and what they will be wearing. If you are having a formal wedding, the photographer and his staff should be dressed as formally as the guests, or at the very least wear black suits. The photographer should also be instructed that at no time should guests' view of the ceremony be blocked. The photographer should work unobtrusively so as not to disrupt the ceremony or the reception.

As with other key vendors, before you settle on a photographer, ask for references of brides with whom the person has worked in the past, and call them to make sure they were happy with the person's work.

Once you've picked a photographer, agree on precisely the style of photography you want–black-and-white, sepia, half black-and-white and half color, traditional, journalistic, documentary, and so on. Provide the photographer with examples of the types of photographs that you want and do not want, clipped from bridal magazines. Review the photographer's book again, and point out what you like as well as what you dislike.

When working with a wedding photographer, scrutinize the fine print in the contract to make sure you understand what's included in the package you're buying and what will cost extra. Will you get to keep your negatives, or will the photographer keep them and charge you for every extra print you request? If so, how much does it cost to purchase the negatives for each and every print? (Although photographers traditionally retained negatives, many will now hand them over to you after you've paid the balance on your bill. After all, your negatives will mean much more to you than they will to him. And you're likely to get much more use out of them in the future to make reprints.) Do you own the proofs, or is there an extra cost to keep them? (Proofs make wonderful gifts to send along with thank-you notes.) Note, however, that with black-and-white photography, prints are usually ordered from contact sheets rather than from separate proofs.

Finally, confirm that the photographer you've chosen will actually be the one photographing your wedding. The fact that another photographer works at the same studio is no guarantee that his work will be of a similar quality or style. Make sure the photographer plans to work through the entire wedding, not just through the ceremony or cake-cutting. And make sure you understand the payment and cancellation policy as well as all the fine print before you sign on the dotted line.

Remember that you, not the photographer, are in charge of the number of formal portraits to be taken. Making portraits of the bridal party is a time-consuming operation. Over the years I have found that most brides and grooms are far happier with one or two great shots of the entire bridal party than with dozens of combinations. Keeping the formal portrait session short allows you to spend time with your guests sharing the joy of the day, and it will also rein in your photography budget. So plan ahead and decide exactly which formal shots you want, make a list, give it to the photographer, and stick to it.

At the wedding you can direct the photographer yourself, but it's more relaxing to ask a trusted friend, your mother, or your maid of honor to work with the photographer to identify everyone and make sure the shots you want are captured. This is like live television–there's no second chance to get a shot of your bridesmaids getting ready, or your little brother all dressed up holding the ring pillow. It is your photographer's responsibility to capture and document the memories that you will want to cherish in the future, but he or she needs your help to do it.

Videographers: What You Need to Know

Many couples hire a videographer to create a living record of their wedding day. A well-produced video can be a wonderful memento of your nuptials. Imagine how interesting it would be now if we could watch a video of our grandmothers walking down the aisle. Today a number of videographers specialize in creating innovative and tasteful wedding videos. Many wedding videos include childhood pictures or home movies of the bridal couple growing up as an introduction, and shots or videos from the honeymoon to conclude. Songs or music that have meaning to the couple can be used as background music. With today's technology there really is no limit to what you can do with a wedding video.

If you choose to work with a videographer, discuss up front what approach you envision. You might want to select a variety of cameras that can lend a grainy, old-fashioned look to parts of the celebration, and blend color footage with black-and-white footage for different effects. You may also want to include a photo montage, and you probably will want to select the music yourselves rather than having the videographer choose for you.

It is important to ascertain ahead of time what kind of lights and equipment the videographer uses and how intrusive the videography will be. It's a shame to exert so much effort to create a romantic and intimate ambience and then have it shattered for the guests with a bright white light suddenly shining in their faces. Take care to select a professional with state-of-the-art equipment that doesn't require extremely bright light or large cameras. If lights must be used, one technique I find helpful is to ask the videographer to hold the camera down with a hand over the light, switch the light on, and then slowly bring the camera up while removing their hand gradually, to avoid suddenly blinding guests with the light.

I also recommend documenting the ceremony from afar, with a microphone on the groom's lapel to capture the sound, so that the videography doesn't interfere with the intimacy of the ritual. Another option is to have a stationary camera installed before the ceremony in an area where a photographer's presence would be intrusive, such as inside a *chuppah* or arbor.

Always discuss beforehand whether you want candid interviews with your guests included. I personally dislike this technique because it's disruptive for guests to be engrossed in conversation one moment, and the next to find lights and a microphone shoved in front of them. It also tends to result in insincere and awkward comments when people are put on the spot.

Music

Since music is the ultimate mood-maker, it's very important to determine what kind of mood you want to set before you choose your wedding music. Think creatively. Don't hire the same type of ten-piece band that you've seen at every other wedding. If your fiancé is of Scottish descent, you could honor his family by hiring a bagpiper to play as guests enter the reception setting. If you're planning a contemporary cocktail party, you might choose a jazz trio. Or you might decide you'd rather spend some time putting together several hours of your favorite music–ask a friend who knows music as well as how to handle stereo equipment to act as your deejay. Another option is to select several different types of music such as a string quartet to play during the ceremony, a trio during cocktails, and a swing band for dancing later on.

If you do decide to hire a band, I recommend going to see them perform rather than simply listening to a tape they've provided. Watch them in action. Are they able to pick up the pace of the party if it starts to lag? Is the bandleader or singer charismatic enough to create a positive rapport with the audience? Will the band's personality and style work for your wedding? If you're planning a sophisticated, black-tie reception, you wouldn't want to walk in and find the bandleader giving guests a lesson in how to perform the electric slide or country-western dance steps!

Because band members often change, it's a good idea to include in the contract the name of the lead singer and certainly to check in with the band a few weeks before the wedding to make sure they haven't suddenly switched to a funk drummer or a jazz-influenced singer who will change the sound of the band dramatically. Finally, be sure to provide the bandleader with a list of songs you definitely *do not* want to hear as well as those you do.

Plan ahead to create some excitement with your music. A bride and groom I recently worked with made a grand entrance into their reception with a procession of violinists leading guests from the ceremony to the dance floor and accompanying the band for the first dance. If you can't afford the string section of the Philharmonic, hire four students from a local music academy or chamber music group to create a similar effect.

Helpful Hints

• Bands often invite a number of friends, assistants, and family members to weddings where they are performing. Specify exactly who and how many people from the band's entourage will be allowed to attend your wedding, what they can wear, when they should arrive, when they can eat and drink, whether they are permitted to smoke, and so on to avoid misunderstandings on your wedding day. Some booking agents may also invite prospective clients to drop by your wedding to watch the band perform. If you have a problem with this, let your booking agent know in advance.

• Avoid "assembled bands." This means that the members don't play together regularly; they've simply been assembled for your event. It also means they may not be accustomed to performing as a group, so chances are they will pause between every song to discuss what to play next and the momentum of the music will be lost. A great song creates lots of great energy on the dance floor, but if the music stops for more than a few moments, the dance floor clears. Hire a band in which the members work together consistently and can play continuously without stopping after each song to regroup.

• I have found it helpful to create a list of rules that can be distributed to all vendors and their workers in advance of the wedding. The list should cover issues such as smoking, areas that are off-limits, what to eat, where to park, and any other concerns. A mutual understanding of your expectations will help ensure a smoother working relationship and fewer surprises on the day of the wedding.

Creating the Schedule of Events–The Most Valuable Tool of the Trade

As in life, the quality of time spent at a party is much more important than the quantity of time. It doesn't matter how much money you spend on flowers, or whether Tom Jones is singing at your wedding or chef Emeril Lagasse is preparing your menu. If your wedding is not well produced–in other words, if it does not have a good sense of timing–your guests will not experience the celebration as you envisioned. Think of your wedding as a journey with a clearly thought-out beginning, middle, and end. Before anyone has a chance to look at a watch, the next activity should take place.

I make a pact with every bride I work with that she will walk down the aisle no more than fifteen to twenty minutes after the ceremony time on the invitation. I also ensure that the cocktail reception lasts no longer than forty-five minutes to an hour to maintain a sense of rhythm and flow to the party.

Good timing is the *most* important, and least expensive, element of any wedding. The tool you use to coordinate this is a schedule of events. This is a typed or handwritten document with a day-by-day, minute-by-minute accounting of *everything* that happens the day before, the day of, and the day after the wedding. Preparing this schedule will help you make sure that all the elements you want are included and will enable you to identify and eliminate any time lags or scheduling problems.

Each person involved in the wedding and reception should be provided with a schedule to ensure that they all know exactly what is planned and when. Go over the schedule with your vendors and bridal party in advance so that any changes or concerns can be addressed well ahead of your wedding day.

I developed the following schedule for a church wedding with a reception at a club on a Sunday. Because the reception site would not permit access to the ballroom until the day of the reception, the installation of the decor began at one minute past midnight on the morning of the wedding day.

Friday

Gift baskets of fresh fruit and chocolate delivered to guest hotel rooms with welcome note, weekend itinerary, map to rehearsal dinner

Saturday

5:00 P.M.	Water and glasses ready for guests attending the wedding rehearsal
5:30 P.M.	Rehearsal at church
7:00 P.M.	Rehearsal over. Guests proceed to restaurant for dinner.

Sunday

12:01 A.M.	Installation of decor begins at reception site: carpeting, drapery, wall panels
10:00 A.M.	Croissants, fruit, mineral water, and juice ready for bride and bridesmaids
	Florist delivers to reception site and begins installation
10:45 A.M.	Florist delivers to setup room at church and begins floral arch
11:00 A.M.	Bridesmaids arrive at bride's home
	Assistant arrives with dresses
	Makeup artists and hairstylist arrive for bride, bridesmaids
12:00 P.M.	Lunch delivered from bride's favorite restaurant and served to bride, mother, and bridesmaids
12:30 P.M.	Photographer arrives at bride's home for shots of everyone getting ready
1:00 P.M.	Photos of bride, mother and father, and bridesmaids
	Personal flowers delivered to home
	Lunch is served to groom and groomsmen at hotel
1:30 P.M.	Choir arrives for rehearsal
2:00 P.M.	Photographer finishes bridesmaid shots, proceeds to church for groom and groomsmen
	Limo 1: arrives for bride and her father
	Limo 2: arrives for bridesmaids
	Videographer arrives
2:15 P.M.	Limo 1: departs for church with bride and her father
	Limo 2: departs for church with bridesmaids
	Bridal dressing room at church set with water and fresh fruit
2:30 P.M.	Limo 1: arrives at church with bride and her father, then returns to bride's home for another pickup
	Limo 2: arrives at church with bridesmaids, then to hotel for another pickup

2:40 P.M.	Groom and groomsmen arrive at church
	Groomsmen photo session
	Sign-in table with guest book ready in entryway of church
2:45 P.M.	Limo 1: arrives at bride's home to pick up other members of wedding party
	Sommeliers arrive at club
2:50 P.M.	Limo 2: arrives at hotel for others in wedding party
2:55 P.M.	Limo 1: leaves for church with others in wedding party
3:00 P.M.	Limo 2: departs hotel for church
	Choir in place
	Quartet in place
3:00 P.M.	Candles ready, bow tied across aisle, reserved seating cards on chairs
	Wedding cake delivered to reception site
	Videographer ready
3:10 P.M.	Limo 1: arrives at church
3:15 P.M.	Limo 2: arrives at church
	Choir begins
	Groomsmen to waiting area
3:30 P.M.	Invitation time—guests are seated from sides
3:35 P.M.	Groomsmen to leave waiting area and move to front of church for entrance
3:45 P.M.	Ceremony commences
	Procession music: Beethoven's "Romance"–played by string quartet
	Grandmothers escorted down aisle and seated in first row
	Parents of groom down aisle
	Bride's mother down aisle
	Minister, groom, and best man proceed from choir door
	Groomsmen
	Bridesmaids
	Matron of honor
	Two ring bearers down aisle
	Two flower girls down aisle
	Church bells
	Music: Kenny G's "Wedding Song"
	Bride and father down aisle
	Ritual commences:
	Lord's Prayer

Reading

Choir to sing after reading

Bride's mother and groom's mother to light candles

Recessional: "Eine Kleine Nachtmusik" (Mozart)

Area set for chorus with fruit juice, water, and fruit

4:15 P.M.	Bridal party proceeds to waiting area
	Guests depart church
4:25 P.M.	Bridal party to altar for formal photo session
	Videographers ready at ceremony area for a few minutes
	Piano, bass, and sax in place at reception site
4:45 P.M.	Limos depart church for reception site–don't forget bridal clothing and handbags
4:50 P.M.	Limos arrive at reception site
4:55 P.M.	Parents join cocktail reception
5:10 P.M.	Bride and groom photo session on grounds of reception site
5:20 P.M.	Full band in place and playing in ballroom
5:30 P.M.	Guests are escorted to ballroom
5:45 P.M.	Band announces bride and groom
	First dance: "Have I Told You Lately"
	Parents of bride and groom invited to join
	Bridal party invited to join
	Family and friends invited to join
	Guests invited to join–music to be upbeat
6:15 P.M.	Wine and water served
	Guests are invited to be seated
6:30 P.M.	First course is served
	Music–background only, five minutes
6:35 P.M.	Music breaks
	Father of bride makes welcome speech
6:37 P.M.	Music–background only
6:50 P.M.	Second course is served
7:05 P.M.	Music to pick up beat–build to first peak
7:35 P.M.	Main course is served
	Music–background only
8:00 P.M.	Music: Father-daughter dance–"To Sir With Love"
	Music changes to upbeat with vocal and builds to second peak

8:50 P.M.	Cake cutting–bride and groom speak
9:00 P.M.	Dessert and cake are served
9:10 P.M.	Music picks up tempo for final peak
9:45 P.M.	Bouquet toss
	Limo 1: arrives for bride and groom
	Limo 2: arrives for parents
10:00 P.M.	Limo 1: bride and groom depart for hotel
	Limo 2: parents, grandparents depart
10:10 P.M.	Guests begin to depart
	Band finishes; quiet recorded background music commences

Monday

8:00 A.M.	Load out begins
	Liquor store collects leftover beverages
8:30 A.M.	Lighting company dismantles lighting
	Florist removes floral vessels and props
9:00 A.M.	Rental company removes rentals

And Last But Not Least . . .

Relax and have fun. The planning process should not overwhelm you. In fact, I encourage you to enjoy every minute of it. Rather than rush out after a frazzling day at the office to try on twenty gowns an hour before the bridal salon closes, set aside a window of time to visit the bridal shop, florist, musicians, and everyone else who is an integral part of your party. Make these visits special; instead of wearing your weekend jeans and sneakers, put on your makeup, fix your hair, and dress nicely. The more attractive you look, the better you will feel. Plus, it's a gesture of respect for your vendors, who will respond to the high standards you are setting for your event. If ever a vendor makes you ill at ease or attempts to push you into anything you are uncomfortable with, be assertive and let the vendor know how you feel. And if that doesn't work, look for someone else to provide the service.

Hopefully, this is the only time in your life that you will be making these plans and decisions, so make the most of them. Your wedding is a unique opportunity to share your happiness with those closest to you, and planning for this celebration should be every bit as fun and creative as the event itself.

Chapter 8

Looking Your Best

Wedding Fashion and Grooming

For many brides, the most fun in planning their wedding is the prospect of picking out their wedding dress. Some brides rush to the bridal shop as soon as that engagement band is on their ring finger. Immediately they find the "perfect" dress–before the date, time of day, site, or style of the wedding has been determined. In the many years that I've been doing weddings, I can't tell you how many times I have run into brides who had to purchase a second and sometimes even a third replacement gown when the others turned out to be wrong for the type of wedding they eventually planned. I cannot stress enough how important it is to wait to purchase your gown until you have decided on the season, the time of day, the site, and the level of formality of your wedding.

Not long ago I worked with a bride who ended up buying *three* gowns as a result of pressure from those around her. The first, her mother convinced her to buy. The second, her maid of honor loved. In both instances the salesperson sided with the mother and the maid of honor, convincing the hapless bride to purchase the dress. Finally she selected a third dress–one that she truly loved and wore for her wedding. As we all know, there is virtually no market for used wedding dresses, and it is a waste to spend money on a collection of gowns you can't use. Don't buy what your mother, your fiancé, your maid of honor, or anyone else thinks is fabulous. They won't be the one wearing it. Find a dress you love and that makes you feel comfortable as well as beautiful.

When you begin to look for a dress, take time to research what is on the market as well as what new styles bridal designers are introducing. I encourage brides to visit at least three different salons or stores and to approach the process of selecting a dress with an open mind. At the start try on a variety of cuts, styles, and colors even if you don't think they will work with your body type or skin tone. Often a dress can be magically transformed from the hanger to your body. Many brides end up choosing a style that is completely different from the one they first selected from the display or envisioned themselves wearing. Even if you have had your heart set on a full tulle skirt since you were a young girl, you may decide you want a simpler, sleeker silhouette after seeing what's available.

Ask yourself what style of dress is appropriate for your setting. Will the celebration be indoors or out? At an upscale downtown hotel or at a friend's house on the shore? A chic slip dress with spaghetti straps will look much better at a summer wedding under a tent than an elaborate Southern-belle number. Also, consider whether the fabric will be appropriate and comfortable for the season. A heavy, rich satin may look gorgeous in the fitting room, but on a humid summer day it may be sweltering.

Above all the dress should fit right and be comfortable. You will be wearing your dress the entire day, for photos, dining, dancing, and more. Don't make yourself miserable. When you try the dress on, sit down as you would at dinner. Hold your arms up as you would if you were hugging your father or dancing with your groom. And never buy a dress that is too tight, assuming you'll automatically drop five or ten pounds before the big day. You'll be much happier in a dress that fits you well.

Keep comfort in mind when shopping for shoes, too. If your wedding is typical, you'll need to walk gracefully and stand straight during the ceremony, dance up a storm at the reception, and be on your feet for many, many hours. Choose a flattering heel height, but not one so high that you'll end up tottering around worried about falling down the aisle or twisting your ankle on the dance floor. Try the shoes on while standing facing your groom to ensure that you are comfortable with the height.

I often recommend that brides buy two pairs of shoes—one in the size they normally wear and another a half-size larger. During the weeks before the wedding, wear the shoes around the house in order to break both sizes in and to determine which feels more comfortable. Bring both pairs with you on your wedding day in case your feet swell and you need the larger ones.

Consider what dress style is most flattering to your figure. Women with fuller figures tend to look more attractive in an A-line cut. Simpler styles are generally more becoming to petite women. It is also important to consider what shade of gown will flatter your skin tone, keeping in mind that the lighting in the store where you are purchasing the dress will differ from the lighting at your party. You might even consult with a makeup artist or a firm specializing in matching colors to your skin tone.

Don't just focus on the dress and how it looks on you; remember that you will have a bouquet, jewelry, perhaps gloves, and a veil or other decorative hair ornaments, all of which can create an over-produced look that may be overwhelming. When you look in the mirror with your entire ensemble on, ask yourself whether the end result is exactly how you want to look. Make sure that *you* are wearing the dress, rather than the dress wearing *you*. That could mean removing something from the picture.

Never believe a pushy bridal salon salesperson who warns you that it's "now or never." Someone who's eager to make a commission may try to convince you that you've got to buy your gown today or walk down the aisle in jeans. That is simply not true. With the exception of couture gowns, most wedding dresses can be completed in eight to ten weeks.

As you did for other aspects of the wedding, clip pictures of dresses you like from magazines. Don't feel limited to bridal magazines, but check mainstream fashion magazines as well. Many brides choose elegant ready-to-wear dresses or sophisticated two-piece suits in lieu of traditional wedding gowns. Shop department stores as well as bridal salons to find the dress that's right for you. Even a simple cocktail dress in pale raw silk can look appropriately bridal with a pair of long gloves, a veil, a bouquet, and other accessories. Other options to consider are having a dress custom made, purchasing a vintage gown, or wearing your mother's dress, which can be altered by a dressmaker and accessorized to give it the look you desire.

Encourage your fiancé to look beyond traditional formalwear shops for his attire, too. There's no law saying he and his groomsmen must show up in the traditional black tuxes and bow ties. An elegantly cut black suit with a silk shirt and open collar for an evening wedding, or a cream linen suit for an outdoor daytime wedding, are distinctive and handsome looks for grooms.

Bridesmaid's Dresses

There is one golden rule when it comes to bridesmaids: Never put them in anything that you yourself would not willingly wear to a breakfast, luncheon, cocktail party, or dinner. Be considerate and be realistic. If you have two model-thin bridesmaids and one who is heavy-set, don't choose horizontal stripes or a skin-tight sheath. You'll make your heavier friend miserable. Keep in mind your bridesmaids' comfort, too. If you're planning a summer wedding with an indoor reception in an air-conditioned space, and the dresses you have chosen for your attendants are sexy, bare-shouldered numbers, you might include a wrap or bolero jacket to keep your friends warm.

Many brides today simply ask each of the women in their party to choose a different cocktail dress, or give a swatch of fabric to each woman and ask her to purchase a dress in that color. Another idea that takes into account the different sizes and shapes of your bridesmaids is to select a fabric that you love, and then have dresses made with slightly different neckline and sleeve treatments for each woman.

Bridal Fashion Terms

Gown Styles

Basque: A gown with a fitted bodice and full skirt, with a downward-pointing V at the waist

Ball gown or ballroom style: A gown with a full, round skirt and fitted bodice

Column: As the name suggests, a straight slender gown made of one piece of fabric and with no seam to distinguish the bodice from the skirt

Empire: A gown with a scooped neckline, high waist, and full skirt (the style you see in all the movie adaptations of Jane Austen novels)

Princess cut or A-line: A gown with no seam to distinguish the bodice from the skirt; instead, the seams run straight from under the arms to the skirt, along the sides of the gown

Sheath: A simple, form-fitting gown that follows the natural curves of the body without being tight

Coatdress: As the name suggests, a gown resembling a fitted coat, with sleeves and buttons up the front, often with a full skirt

These terms cover only the basics. Many of the these styles are often modified. For example, a gown might combine a modern mock-turtleneck bodice or a corset-style bodice that laces along the back with a full ballroom-style skirt. You're likely to hear many other terms when you're shopping. It's always a good idea to ask the salesperson to explain the fashion terms that apply to your dress style and accessories. It will help you when describing the overall tone and style of your wedding to your florists and other vendors.

Trains

Sweep: A train that falls on the floor for about six inches

Chapel: Slightly longer than the sweep, a train that extends 12 to 18 inches along the floor

Cathedral: A train that extends 22 or more inches along the floor; usually reserved for formal weddings

Royal or monarch: A train that extends a yard or more on the floor

Train Attachments

Capelet: A train attached at the back shoulder of the dress

Watteau: A train attached at the back yoke of the dress

Veils

Birdcage: A short, chin-length veil

Mantilla: A round veil usually made of lace and worn without a headpiece (often worn in traditional Catholic ceremonies)

Blusher: A sheer veil worn over the face and lifted during the ceremony

Flyaway: A layered, shoulder-length veil

Fingertip: A veil that would reach your fingertips if your arms were relaxed at your sides

Waltz or ballet: A veil that reaches just below your knee

Chapel: A veil that extends one to two feet beyond the gown

Cathedral: A very formal veil that extends two or more feet on the floor, usually worn with a cathedral-style train

Doing the Right Thing: *Who pays for the brides-maids' dresses?*

Tradition held that the bride or her family covered these expenses. It's still a wonderful gesture if you can afford to buy these items, particularly if your friends are already planning to splurge on travel expenses to attend your wedding. However, if your budget doesn't allow you to purchase the bridesmaids' dresses, it *is* acceptable to ask them to pay for their own attire so long as you keep the cost within a reasonable budget (theirs, not yours). If you expect them to pay, it's also crucial that you choose something the women can wear again, perhaps a simple, classic cocktail dress or dinner suit. (Let's be honest: Nobody is going to wear that frilly peach prom-dress style anywhere but a costume party.) Another option is to offer to split the cost with your friends or to buy the accessories, such as shoes and/or jewelry.

If you plan to include children in your wedding party, wait to choose the children's attire until you've selected attire for yourselves and your adult attendants. Think of the children's dresses or suits as the finishing touches. There's no rule that flower girls must wear the same color as the bride, or that ring bearers must wear miniature tuxedos to match the groomsmen.

Since the children will precede you down the aisle and in all likelihood will be posing with you for pictures, choose colors and styles that complement the rest of the wedding party's clothing. Make sure the clothes you choose are comfortable for the children. Avoid skirts so long that a child might trip while walking down the

aisle, and steer clear of anything stiff and itchy. Children can get fidgety enough during a service that lasts longer than five minutes, so avoid dressing them in an outfit that will make them even more restless.

Beauty Strategies for Looking Your Best

I arrange for every bride I work with to have a massage on the morning of her wedding. It's a time that allows her to relax and gather herself in preparation for the day ahead. Usually a manicure and pedicure are also on the schedule. You might consider doing the same for yourself and your maid of honor. Your bridesmaids could probably use a little rest and relaxation on the morning of the wedding, just like you. Even a hand or foot massage for the attendants is a wonderful gesture if your budget allows you to have a masseuse on site.

It is absolutely essential that you arrange for a trial run of your hairstyle and makeup with your wedding attire a few weeks before your wedding. This is not the day to find out that you're allergic to the foundation that the makeup artist uses or to learn that the hairstylist has a more radical vision for your bridal coiffure than you had in mind. Be sure to test the makeup under the same lighting you expect to have at your wedding. It's also a good idea to take a few snapshots to see whether you like the way you look on film. Sometimes what looks great in the salon appears washed out or overdone in pictures. Put on your veil, jewelry, gloves, and accessories to make sure that this is *exactly* how you want to look for your wedding.

The same principle applies to cuts and hair

Preserving Your Wedding Dress

It may be the last thing you want to think of at the time of your wedding, but do consider whether you want your dress professionally preserved so that it will last for generations. If you do, plan ahead by retaining the services of a dry cleaner that specializes in preserving bridal gowns. Have your mother or maid of honor take your dress to the cleaner the first business day after the wedding. Under no circumstances should you try to remove any spills and stains yourself; leave it to the professionals. A bridal-gown-cleaning specialist will ensure your dress is properly cleaned and packaged with tissue so that it will look just as beautiful years from now as it did when you walked down the aisle.

Beauty Tips

Hair and makeup artists Laura Geller of New York and Kris Levine of Los Angeles are expert in helping brides look their very best. Following are several of their suggestions for bridal beauty:

• Arrange for beauty treatments such as facials and waxing no less than two weeks prior to your wedding, so that your skin will have time to recover from any irritation.

• Use makeup remover to take off all your makeup the night before your wedding, then don't use it again on your wedding day. Makeup removers can irritate your skin, and leftover residue will prevent cosmetics from setting well.

• Opt for water-resistant mascara rather than waterproof mascara. Waterproof mascara is more likely to cake or clump.

• If you have any skin allergies or sensitivities, tell your makeup artist about them well ahead of time in order to allow her to find makeup suited to your particular needs. Any new products or cosmetics to be used on your wedding day should be tested on your skin two weeks ahead to be sure you are not sensitive to them.

• If you are planning a summer wedding, apply sunblock under your makeup even if you plan to spend only a short time outdoors. Choose lightweight foundation that will allow your skin to breathe and that will be less likely to run, and avoid heavy perfumes or makeup that might attract bees.

• Apply a lipstick sealer, *then* apply your lipstick with a brush, and gently pat on loose powder afterward. This will help the lipstick stay fresh and prevent it from leaving a lip print on others.

• Choose creamy rather than matte lipsticks, and matte rather than frosted eye shadows. They look more natural and vibrant in photographs.

• Take a moment to slip away and refresh your makeup as the reception goes on. You'll want to look as fresh and attractive in your photos from the end of the evening as you did in those from the beginning of the day.

• Ignore pressure to use trendy shades of makeup or nail polish, and choose tones that you know from experience will work well with your hair and skin coloring.

• If you have hired a makeup artist to apply your cosmetics and you plan on a formal photo session after the ceremony, ask the person to stay to touch up your makeup prior to the photos. Also, be aware that if your ceremony is in the late afternoon and your reception goes into the evening, you might want to enhance your makeup for evening lighting, which requires different shading and a bit more drama.

coloring. Book hair appointments at least two weeks before the wedding. That way your hair will have a chance to grow out a little and settle into the style. If it's a new style, you'll give yourself a chance to get used to it. If the color isn't right, you'll have time for it to be corrected. I also advise brides to wash their hair the evening before the wedding rather than the morning of; it makes the hair look fuller and gives it more body. If you are having a stylist arrange your hair before the ceremony, make sure he or she stays until after the ceremony to help you remove your veil, if desired, and give your hair a last-minute touch-up.

Helpful Hints

• Stay out of the sun and especially the tanning salon right before your wedding. A sunburn could be disastrous on the wedding day.

• Keep a compact with pressed powder in your purse or dressing room so you can reapply before major photo opportunities.

Remember your bridesmaids. I think it is a generous gesture for a bride to arrange and pay for their hair and makeup sessions the day of the wedding. It ensures that all your bridesmaids are on time for the wedding. It will give a more unified, finished look to the bridal party, and all the bridesmaids will feel more confident. Finally, it's so much fun for you to have your hair and makeup done together; it's a wonderful time to reminisce and enjoy each other. While it's ideal to have a hair and makeup professional come to the bride's home or the wedding site, a salon can be less expensive.

Thank you for making the journey. We want this to be a beautiful and memorable weekend as we join together to share our love, our passion and our friendship with each other, and with you.

As part of our wedding ceremony, we want to include you into our eternal memory of this special occasion. Enclosed you will find a piece of ribbon and pen. We would like for you to write down your best wishes and bring it with you to the ceremony on Saturday. Your ribbons will be placed at the alter as we bind our love together forever. After the ceremony, your wishes will be placed in a special box that will be opened on our first anniversary and will serve as a keep sake of this joyous occasion.

Our celebration begins on Friday evening at 8:00 pm. Please meet at the beach in front of the Ocean Club.

On Saturday, please join us again at the beach in front of the Ocean Club at 6:30 pm for our wedding ceremony. Cocktails and dinner to follow.

For a final farewell, meet us at the Versailles Garden level before the Lilly Pond at 11:00 am for a brunch.

This is a special time for us and we hope that for you it will be equally special.

Much Love,

Natasha and Matt

Chapter 9

The Wedding Day

Being a Gracious Bride

I have said before that your wedding day should be about you and your groom, and I firmly believe that. But your celebration is also about your guests–the most important people in your lives–and making sure they share in your joy. There are a number of things that you can do on your wedding day to communicate to your friends and family how precious they are to you and how much you care about their happiness. Here are a number of ideas to consider for your celebration.

• If your ceremony will include any rituals or customs that guests might find unfamiliar–the Jewish breaking of the glass, the unity candle, and so on–include a paragraph in your program explaining how the ritual came about and why it is significant to you. If you are not printing a program, print the information from your computer in a beautiful font and place a sheet on each guest's seat at the ceremony.

• A thoughtful bridal couple will go to the trouble of creating a seating plan for the reception. Even if you don't plan to have a formal sit-down dinner with place cards, I suggest at the very least that you indicate at which tables you would like groups of people to sit. There's nothing worse than having one or two people end up at a table alone while others pull chairs away to crowd up to a more popular table. Another great way to honor your guests is to place a silver picture frame on each table with the names of all the guests seated at that particular table. That way you can ensure that groups of friends will have a chance to catch up, as well as introduce guests who've never met.

• Designate smoking and nonsmoking areas, and make sure that the catering staff enforces the smoke-free zones.

• Always include a nonalcoholic beverage that is served along with glasses of champagne or cocktails, to accommodate guests who do not drink alcohol or who wish to skip a round.

• Choose a menu that reflects your tastes, but that's not too exotic for your guests to eat. For example, if you're opposed to eating red meat, don't assume your guests will love an all-sushi appetizer list and Chilean sea bass for dinner just because you do. Offer as an alternative a more mainstream dish such as a pasta or chicken.

• Consider having a calligraphied or printed menu placed on each table or at each place setting so guests are aware of what is being served.

• Be sensitive to guests' feelings and personalities. Some single women are embarrassed at the thought of being dragged onto the dance floor for the ceremonial bouquet toss. If someone doesn't want to participate, don't force them. In fact, if your best man is painfully shy, you might ask your

Ladies' Room Amenities

Antacid tablets or liquid for indigestion*

Aspirin*

Band-Aids*

Bobby pins

Chewing gum, breath mints, and mouthwash*

Clear nail polish (for mending runs in nylons)

Dental floss*

Facial tissues*

Hairbrush and comb*

Hair spray

Hand lotion or moisturizing cream*

Lip balm*

Nail file and emery board*

Pantyhose (one or two extra pairs for emergencies in neutral colors)

Pens and sticky notes*

Safety pins

Sanitary napkins and tampons

Sewing kit

* These items should be stocked in a basket or on a shelf of the men's room as well as the ladies' room.

gregarious maid of honor who is an aspiring actress to make the first toast instead. Give the best man a substitute responsibility that suits him so he won't feel slighted.

• During the reception make an effort to spend a few moments with each guest and to find something sincere and personal to say. I dislike receiving lines since they seem artificial and insincere. Also, they tend to bottle up the entrance to the reception areas and can waste a lot of time, causing your party to lose its natural momentum. Instead, I encourage brides and grooms to circulate among the tables after they've eaten dinner or during dessert to ensure that they have the opportunity to greet everyone. You and your groom can also greet a number of guests at the cocktail hour after photos are taken, should time allow. Or schedule most of your photos before the ceremony to leave more time for socializing during your cocktail hour.

The most important advice I can offer you is very simple: Do not waste the precious hours of your wedding day worrying or getting upset because the roses are ivory instead of champagne or because the deejay played the song that was at the top of your list to avoid. Remember that the real significance of your wedding day is the commitment you are making to the man you love and the fact that the most important people in both of your lives have gathered around you to share in your happiness. Everything else is icing on the cake.

Welcoming Out-of-Town Guests

When guests have traveled a distance to attend your wedding, you of course want to welcome them and thank them for sharing in your celebration. At a typical wedding, however, it's difficult, if not impossible, for the bride and groom to personally welcome all their out-of-town guests, particularly those who are staying at hotels. A lovely substitute is a welcome note from the bride and groom, perhaps tied with a beautiful ribbon and some dried flowers, that can be delivered to the hotel ahead of time and placed in the guests' rooms before they check in. The note should welcome the guests and thank them for traveling to attend the wedding, and provide all the scheduling information and details the guests will need to have a wonderful time at your celebration. Accompanying the note with a welcome basket or nicely wrapped gift is a lovely touch, too. You don't need to spend a lot of money; something small and thoughtful will be appreciated. Here are some ideas for filling a welcome basket:

Fine chocolates or chocolate-covered strawberries

Bath salts, bubble bath, or other fragrant bath products

Wine or champagne

Mineral water

Flowers

Fresh fruit

Cheese and a variety of crackers or a fresh baguette

Freshly baked cookies

Croissants and gourmet coffee

A guidebook and map of the city

A voucher for a city tour, if they'll be spending the weekend

A list of your favorite local shops, restaurants, and sights to help them fill their free hours

Dear Deborah and Roy
Our sincerest thanks for
the very beautiful

Chapter 10

A Million Thanks

Sending Personalized Thank-You Letters

Your wedding guests are your nearest and dearest friends and relatives–the most important people in the world to you as a couple. You've chosen them above everyone else to share one of the most special days of your life. Your guests, in turn, may have traveled many miles, taking time off from their own jobs and their own lives to be with you. In most cases each of your guests has put time and thought into selecting a beautiful wedding gift to please you and your groom. Letting your guests know you appreciate their sharing your celebration and their wonderful gift is one of your most important responsibilities as a new couple. A simple, heartfelt, and sincere thank-you note takes only minutes to write and costs almost nothing, yet it means so much.

Not long ago I designed and planned a party in New York for actress Nicole Kidman. Nicole was in town on a very tight, busy schedule and was leaving at noon the following day for a trip abroad. The party was a great success, which was very satisfying to me. But I was so impressed the following morning, when despite her busy schedule, at ten A.M. a hand-written, sincere, and eloquent thank-you note from Nicole was delivered to my home. This is the kind of gesture that separates a gracious, thoughtful person from the rest.

Unfortunately, thank-you notes cause many brides (and many people in general, for that matter) unnecessary anxiety. They put off writing because they don't know exactly what to say or because they envision having to write 150 thank-you notes all at once. Actually thank-you notes are a much easier part of the wedding process than choosing your dress or your flowers. And once you get used to writing thank-you notes , you'll be amazed at how simple it is to write a gracious and heartfelt note for absolutely every occasion.

When to Write Them

No one expects you to spend your honeymoon churning out ten-page novellas to every single wedding guest, or putting a cloud over your first week home as husband and wife by insisting that you both write several dozen thank-you notes daily.

But shortly after you return home from your honeymoon, it is important to tackle the task of the thank-you notes. As a general rule of thumb, you should plan to respond to a gift within six weeks of receiving it–and of course, sooner whenever possible. So if you receive something from a long-distance friend two months before your wedding, don't wait to thank her until after the wedding; do it right away.

One of the simplest ways to stay organized is to keep a running list of all the gifts you receive as they arrive. Working from the master guest list, jot down the name of the person who sent the gift, what the gift was, when you received it, and a comment or two about it ("hand-painted blue-and-white pottery; reminds me of our trip to New England; will look nice on kitchen windowsill"). Check each person's name off the list as you finish a thank-you to them. At all costs, you want to avoid thanking someone for the wrong gift or making it obvious in your note that you don't remember exactly what was sent. Sometimes mistakes happen, but most can be avoided by being organized from the outset. Another helpful idea is to take a Polaroid photo of each gift as it is opened. Again, jot down the name of the person who sent the gift and the date you received it on the back of the photo. Remember, even if you've thanked someone in person or on the phone, you should still send a handwritten note.

There's no need to tackle all your notes in one interminable writing marathon. Make things easy on yourself by finding a comfortable space to write and concentrating on only five or six thank-yous a day. Perhaps complete one or two at lunch every day and a few in the evening before bed. Before you know it, you'll have them all written, and you will have been able to focus on making each one fresh and personal.

Doing the Right Thing: *Can I type my thank-you notes or print them out on the computer?*
Only if you have handwriting like a doctor. Thank-you notes should always be handwritten because they are personal. Today, when we all have access to personal computers, a handwritten note has even more impact, and I believe it is a tradition to cherish. Only if you truly have illegible handwriting is it acceptable to type a thank-you note, and the note should always include a quick word of apology explaining why you have chosen to type it. Choosing a typeface that looks like script is a step in the right direction.

In composing your notes, try to think of something special to say to each person. First, focus on the person, then on the gift. Mention the item specifically and what you plan to use it for. ("Thank you so much for the beautiful Haute Couture champagne glasses from Lenox. We can't wait to have you over for cocktails so we can enjoy them together!") You might also mention how the gift will fit into your home and your lifestyle. ("The crystal clock you sent looks beautiful on the mantel. It matches our decor exquisitely and really helped to complete the look of our living room.") If the gift wasn't some-thing you requested or particularly like, focus instead on how nice it was to see the person at your wedding.("Thank you so much for the lovely dish towels. We were so happy that you two could make the trip from Seattle to share in our special day. It meant so much to us to have you be a part of our wedding.") If you got to spend a few special moments together during the wedding, you might mention that. ("It was so much fun to see all of our old college roommates together again. Laughing and talking with you at the cocktail party brought back so many fun memories and made the day so special. Let's plan to get everyone together again this summer.") For gifts of cash or a check, describe what you plan to spend the money on. ("Thank you so much for your very generous check. Jim and I plan to put it toward a painting we've had our eye on for quite a while.")

Thank-you notes can be short. The point is to make them warm and personal. There's no need to be formal and no need to agonize over what to write. No one will go over your note with a fine-tooth comb to find misspellings or correct your grammar; they'll simply be touched and happy that you remembered them.

Do, however, make sure you've spelled everyone's name correctly. That goes for wives and husbands of extended guests, too. If you're unsure about the spelling of someone's name, check the spelling against your master guest list.

Immediately after the whirlwind of the wedding has ended, your mind will be full of images and memories. In the rush to go off on your honeymoon, don't forget to thank the most important people who played a role in your wedding. That might be your maid of honor, your wedding consultant, or even your parents. Trust me: If you had a wonderful wedding and are overwhelmed with feelings of gratitude and love toward your parents, it will mean the world to them if you put your thoughts down on paper. Here are some examples.

To parents:

Dear Mom and Dad,

Jason and I have just arrived in Bali and we spent the last nineteen hours talking about our wedding and reliving every moment, from the time the first guests arrived at the rehearsal dinner to the time we left for our honeymoon. We had the most extraordinary evening. It was everything we ever wanted it to be! I cannot begin to thank you enough for all that you have taught me and done to prepare me for this moment. Thank you for the values you instilled in me and for all the opportunities you have given me. I know Jason and I now have the opportunity to create a relationship like the two of you enjoy. We look forward to seeing you and sharing our pictures when we get back.

Much love,

Marianne

To your maid of honor:

Dear Gloria,

Words cannot quite adequately express how grateful I am for all that you did to help me with my wedding plans. You really redefined the meaning of the word *friendship*. I can't thank you enough for keeping me calm when I was worried, for reassuring me when I was nervous, and for just being such a true friend. Of course, I love the personalized stationery you sent, which now allows me to write such elegant notes. It's in my favorite color, and I love the embossing. You certainly know my taste! Thanks again and I look forward to our continued relationship.

With much love,

Jean

To your wedding consultant:

Dear Stuart,

Thank you so much for working so closely with Dennis and me to create the wedding that we have always envisioned. The phone has not stopped ringing–every single one of our guests thoroughly enjoyed themselves, and we got to party, too. Thank you for being so generous with your time and your knowledge and for guiding me when I was having problems making decisions. I hope you do baby showers! That's probably the next time I'm going to be throwing a big party. We look forward to having you over to share our wedding photos with you very soon.

With much appreciation,

Emily and Brian

Helpful Hints

• You might want to consider having note cards printed in the same style as your invitations with your name and your husband's name at the top or your monogrammed initials.

• Avoid preprinted thank-you cards that say "Thank you for the _____." They are in the worst possible taste and insulting to your guests, who took time to choose a wedding gift just for you.

• A photo of the guest taken at the wedding is a wonderful enclosure to a thank-you note. Or send a wedding photo of you and your husband or your entire family for friends and family members who sent a gift but couldn't attend. If you have a lot of extra proofs that you don't need, this is a good way to use them; or you can have one favorite photo duplicated in quantity.

Doing the Right Thing: *Who should write the wedding thank-you notes? Me, my husband, or both of us? How can I convince him to help? Should notes be signed from both of us or one?*

This is one of those tasks that will help you learn to work together and divide responsibilities–the first of many you'll encounter now that you're married. Try dividing the thank-you notes, with each of you writing to the guests you know best or who sent gifts specific to one of your tastes or interests. Certainly the best man and groomsmen will find a note from your husband more meaningful than one written by you. Likewise, your maid of honor and close female friends will prefer a note from you. You can sign your notes from one or both of you.

Doing the Right Thing: *What do I do if I want to return a gift? And if I do return the gift, how do I thank the person who sent it? Can I call and ask them where they got the gift so I'll know where to return it?*
If you decide to return a gift, send a gracious note thanking the giver and letting them know that you've exchanged it for something you really love. ("Thank you so much for the lovely waffle iron. You know how much we always enjoy making Sunday brunch at home. To our surprise, we received two of them, so we fortunately managed to exchange your thoughtful gift for a juicer which we expect to use frequently. Can't wait to have you over to enjoy brunch with us soon.")

However, it is impolite to ask a person who has sent you a gift where they bought the item because you want to return it. If you are not able to return the gift on your own, it's better to write a courteous thank-you note and simply tuck the gift away for later, and use it when the friends who sent it to you come to your home.

Doing the Right Thing: *What if several people sent a gift as a group? Can I send one thank-you to the group or should I send individual notes?*
If it's possible to write to them all at one location, then go ahead and send a group thank-you. If several coworkers threw you a shower, for example, a thank-you note to the office, along with a group gift such as a basket of muffins or cookies, is a gracious gesture.

Doing the Right Thing: *What do I do if I didn't receive a gift from one of my guests? Should I write a note thanking them for attending? Should I ask them about the gift in case it might have gotten lost?*
Never call to ask whether someone sent a gift. It's presumptuous. Guests have up to a year after your wedding to send a gift without breaching rules in anybody's etiquette book. There is no need to send a thank-you note to a guest simply for attending the wedding, unless you feel a real closeness to the person or they did something special for you at the event.

Thank-You Notes for Any Occasion
Thank-you notes aren't just for weddings. Many of the above ideas and guidelines apply to thank-yous for birthdays, holiday gifts, and other occasions as well as weddings. However, there is an art to the everyday thank-you. Here are a few hints to get you started.

Be prompt. Set a pattern for yourself of writing thank-yous within a day of receiving gifts, being hosted at someone's house, and so on, *and stick to it*. It might seem difficult at first, but before long it becomes a habit as automatic as brushing or flossing your teeth. Get into the routine of writing thank-you notes regularly–when someone takes you out for dinner or gives you a gift. Whenever someone makes a special gesture for you, they deserve a thank-you note in return.

Whenever I travel, I carry several sheets of stationery or personalized note cards with me. After an evening at a friend's house or a dinner party, I write a thank-you as soon as I get back to my hotel room, while the evening is still fresh in my mind. Then I always mail it before I check out of the hotel. It takes only a few minutes of my time; it makes a good impression on the recipient, and it's simply the right thing to do.

Tuck a few thank-you cards and a small address book into your purse or luggage when you travel. And always make sure to get your hosts' address before you leave their home. I often travel up to four or five days a week, and I always bring along a few thank-you cards or my personal stationery. For me, airplane travel is a great time to write.

Don't forget about thank-yous for business associates and friends at the office. For example, if your boss takes you out to lunch around the holidays, write a thank-you even if holiday lunches are considered an "office tradition" or if you're treated to lunch as a group.

When You're Too Busy to Write

The last thing I want to do is to load you down with written-in-stone absolutes that must be followed. My goal is simply to help you come up with guidelines that are socially appropriate and that–most important–work for you. If you're too busy to write thank-yous, or if the mere thought of writing brings on a panicky flashback to English Composition 101, send an e-mail, fax a note, or leave a voice-mail message at the very least. Although weddings are one of the few very special occasions for which it's imperative that you send a written thank-you note to every guest who sent you a gift, in most other circumstances an e-mail message, a phone call, or another type of informal thank-you is quite acceptable. After all, we're living in the electronic age–why not update our etiquette to match our technology?

Think back to the last time you hosted a party: Remember when you were reflecting, as you straightened up the next day, hoping your guests enjoyed themselves? Think how reassuring it was when friends called to tell you what a fun time they had. Do the same for others who are thoughtful enough to invite you over for dinner or to a cocktail party.

Sample Thank-you Notes

To wedding guests:

Dear Margaret and Nevins,

We thoroughly enjoyed having you be part of our wedding celebration. Thank you so much for the beautiful cake server. We shall treasure it always.

Much love,

Nick and Kathy

Dear Leigh Anne and Michael,

It was great to see you at our wedding. We had so much fun and are so happy that you could spend our special day with us. Thank you for the lovely set of colorful towels. We look forward to using them in the summertime around the pool.

Much love,

Janet

Dear Gordon and Karen,

We thoroughly enjoyed the time we spent with you during our wedding celebration. So glad you could make it. Thank you for the wonderful set of martini glasses. We shall think of you every evening when we enjoy a relaxing cocktail.

Much love,

Mitchell and Lyneale

To a group of coworkers:

To Charlene, Jill, Jane, and Jacqui,

Thank you so much for creating such a wonderful shower. I feel so blessed to work with such caring friends. I am extremely grateful for all your support and for putting up with me when I was distracted by wedding plans for the past three months! The shower was wonderful, and I appreciate all your efforts as well as the beautiful gifts.

With much love,

LuLu

After a dinner party:

Dear David and Lisa,

We had so much fun last night. The food was incredibly delicious, the flowers were gorgeous, the wine superb, and most of all, we enjoyed meeting new people and spending time with you. Thank you for including us.

Much love,

Tom and Lisa

Dear Debbie and Paul,

Thank you so much for the wonderful dinner last night. As usual, whenever we're with you we have a great time. The food was exceptional, and I'm so glad you sat me next to Margo. We got on famously, and I made a new friend. I look forward to seeing you next week.

Much love,

Jocelyn

Dear Karyn and Joel,

Thank you so much for hosting the lovely dinner to introduce us to your friends. We're so happy to be part of the community, and we look forward to spending much more time with you and all the wonderful new friends we met at your house this week.

Much love,

Vanessa and Rick

Another important type of note to learn how to write is a letter of condolence. When friends are grieving over the loss of a loved one, they will value and appreciate your support and caring thoughts more than ever. Even if you are worried that you won't say precisely the right thing, the gracious gesture is to write a brief message simply letting your friend know you are thinking of them. Express your sadness on their behalf, refer to the person who passed away, and offer your help and support if they need you. You might also consider sending flowers or a donation to a charity in the name of the person who passed away. Another thoughtful gesture is to send a basket of fruit, a dessert, or a deli tray to the family's home when you know people will be dropping by to offer their condolences. And of course, make an effort to attend the funeral.

Dear Christine,

My deepest sympathies are with you at this time. I was very sad to hear of the untimely loss of your grandmother. I know what a great influence she was on you and how close you were. If I can be of any assistance to you in any way, please don't hesitate to call me at any time.

With much love and sympathy,

Michelle

Conversely, if the funeral was in your family or circle of friends, make an effort to acknowledge those who expressed sympathy and support by sending them a thank-you note. Don't forget to thank clergy members, friends who spoke at the funeral, pallbearers, and so on.

Chapter 11

Gift-Giving–*From* the Bride

D id the caterer design a special seafood dish just for you and your groom, to reflect the first meal you ever had together? Did a friend run out at the last minute to buy disposable cameras for the tables or extra satin ribbon for the bouquets? Did your wedding co-ordinator manage to find just the right antique silver frames and candlesticks you had envisioned for the centerpieces? Did the best man make an especially moving toast? Why not send them a small gift to express your gratitude?

A personal gift to those who have helped make your wedding special is a wonderful token of appreciation. These gifts needn't be expensive; a nice bottle of champagne or wine; an attractive flowering plant or orchid in a decorative container; or a small gift basket of cheese and fruit, aromatic soaps and bath items, or specialty coffees and chocolates, with a short note attached, will certainly be appreciated.

Consider sending gifts *before* the wedding to people who are making extra efforts to help you. If it's within your budget, send a note and some chocolates to your hairdresser after you have had a trial run thanking her for her efforts and letting her know how much confidence you have placed in her for your wedding day. I always send a cash gratuity or a bottle of wine or champagne to the chef and the maître d' before the wedding. It goes a long way as an incentive to ensure a delicious dinner.

Of course, you will be presenting a gift to each of your bridesmaids with a note thanking them for their support in planning your wedding and letting them know how much you value their friendship. You might also consider a similar gift for your parents and your groom's parents to thank them for their help.

Don't forget your fiancé. Grooms often tend to feel slightly overlooked with so much attention focused on the bride leading up to the wedding. The morning of your wedding is a wonderful time to have a gift delivered to your groom by the best man or wedding coordinator. The gift can be anything you think he'll love, from a vintage watch, to an heirloom pair of cuff links that belonged to your grandfather, to tickets to his favorite sporting event, to a box of fine cigars or a humidor, to a beautiful book of poetry with a special inscription from you.

Tips on Sending Gifts

Your wedding is an occasion for much giving and receiving of gifts, but the art of gift-giving isn't reserved just for weddings and special occasions. I am a firm believer in buying and sending gifts when the spirit moves you. A gift is a token of friendship that lets friends know you are thinking about them; you don't necessarily need a reason to send a thoughtful message.

I have always loved selecting gifts, and I love receiving them, too. It has nothing to do with the

Bridesmaids' Gifts

The gracious bride selects personal gifts for the women in her wedding party as a thank-you for their help and support. Appropriate gifts range from classics such as jewelry or engraved silver pieces, to fun ideas such as theater tickets or a gift certificate at a favorite restaurant. Use your imagination. If your maid of honor is an aspiring writer, you might present her with a beautiful leather-bound journal or a monogrammed fountain pen. If she's an executive, you might give her an elegant silver business card case with her initials engraved on the top. Here are some ideas to get you thinking.

- Silver, gold, or pearl earrings or bracelets
- Pearl necklace, choker, or pendant
- Engraved silver picture frame
- Crystal decanter, perfume bottle, or bud vase
- Vintage sterling silver hair combs, clips, or barrettes
- Gift certificates for a massage, facial, manicure and pedicure, or day of beauty

dollar value, but everything to do with the thought behind it. I have a very dear friend, Margo Baker-Barbakow, who is extremely thoughtful and generous. She could find a small silver pickle fork while shopping for herself at an antiques market and not think twice of buying it and sending it to me because she knows I love to collect antique silver serving pieces. She prides herself on finding fun and unique personal gifts and also takes a lot of time and thought in wrapping them. I once witnessed her send a birthday gift to a young nephew. She took a simple paper party hat and placed it in a box, then crumpled up dollar bills and wedged them around the hat to protect it. Imagine the expression on the boy's face when he realized the packaging around his party hat was actually a very generous gift! What a great idea.

I send gifts when I want to show friends I care, but I also buy gifts throughout the year when I find them. Often I put gifts away in advance of birthdays and holidays. This strategy eliminates the stress of running around frantically on Christmas Eve or two hours before a birthday party scrambling to find anything passable. Also, by buying appropriate gifts for friends and relatives when you find them, you're much more likely to give truly special, personalized gifts that people will treasure.

If you have certain stores you shop at regularly, consider leaving your personal stationery or note cards with them. I leave mine with the florist, the chocolatier, and the wine shop. This way you can call at the last minute, dictate a note on your stationery, and make a personalized gesture. Aside from personal stationery, many mail-order catalogs offer custom ribbon and note cards that can be printed with "A gift from Tom and Lisa," "With many thanks," "Enjoy," or another message.

I often send gifts to special clients to thank them for their continued business. I've done this for years, and it's amazing how it's paved the way for new business and personal recommendations. If you or your husband has clients or professional associates who are particularly supportive and with whom you work often, consider sending a small gift at the holidays or whenever you feel inclined–perhaps an engraved pen, a desk set, an elegant leather business-card holder, a bottle of champagne, or a fragrant candle. Attach a note thanking them for their business and letting them know how much you look forward to working with them in the future.

Helpful Hints:

• Gorgeous packaging makes a gift even more special, so don't neglect gift wrapping. Keep a good supply of seasonal and nonseasonal gift wrap and ribbon on hand. You can also create a personal signature for your gifts by selecting a single type of paper and ribbon, buying it in bulk, and using it year-round, as your trademark. If you don't have time to wrap gifts yourself, shop at stores that provide the service.

• Remember Secretary's Day, and consider sending a small gift to your secretary as well as your husband's. You'd be surprised at how much a well-chosen gift can cement good relations between you and those professionals that you rely on.

• We've all had the experience of ordering flow-

Host and Hostess Gifts

• A bottle of champagne or vintage wine

• Bottled olive oils or jams

• A bouquet of fresh flowers (sent the day before or after the event, as bringing them with you would force your host to double as a florist rather than greet other guests)

• A designer scented candle or decorative potpourri canister

• A box of gourmet chocolates sent the day before or after the event

ers as a gift via long distance, from a florist whom we don't know. Guard against poor floral design by ordering bouquets made of a single type of flower (in season) en masse. It creates a wonderful effect, and as long as the flowers are in good condition, it is always beautiful–for example, just white roses, or a large bunch of sweet peas. Or you might tell the florist that you are personally going to attend the event that the flowers are being sent to.

• Chocolates are a great gift idea and are also easy to send by mail or air courier. A gift of chocolates can be personalized by including a note on your personal stationery that is given to your chocolatier in advance to include with your gift.

How to Select Personalized Gifts

Giving great gifts is easy–it just takes a little thought. Here's how to do it.

• What types of books and magazines does the person enjoy reading? Magazine subscriptions and books are an easy yet very personal gift. If the person has a favorite author, you might search for a first edition or a signed copy of one of that author's books. Always keep an eye out for book signings; if an author is signing a new coffee-table book or novel, you can get several copies with personal inscriptions and hang on to them for Mother's Day, Father's Day, Christmas, or any other occasion. Note that you don't actually have to attend the signings; call the bookstore in advance and they will be delighted to have the books inscribed for you and held until you pick them up.

• Does the person enjoy cooking or a particular type of cuisine? If so, consider a lovely bottle of olive oil, an unusual wine or vinegar, a specialty cookbook, or a gift certificate to a hot new restaurant.

• Does the person have a vacation planned? Consider giving a book about the destination. For instance, if they're planning a trip to Paris in the spring, they'll probably have basic guidebooks, but perhaps you could buy a special book on Parisian cafés or the city's literary landmarks.

• Does the person collect anything unusual? Antique cigarette cases? Majolica? Items for the garden? Consider adding something special to their collection.

• What is his or her decorating style? What are the dominant colors they use for decorating or for clothing? If someone is doing a house at the beach and their colors are blue and white, a set of napkins, a tablecloth, or a vase in blue and white or a complementary color such as yellow and in a light, airy style befitting a beach home would be very appropriate.

• Is the person a theater buff? Tickets to a play, ballet, opera, or another cultural event make a lovely and personalized gift.

• Is the person a music fan? Perhaps you can find a rare recording of their favorite artist or preferred type of music. A few tapes or CDs wrapped beautifully are always an appropriate gift for music lovers.

• Does the person love to travel? Mileage certificates or an upgrade to first class make wonderful gifts (especially for honeymoon couples).

Doing the Right Thing: *Who is responsible for remembering birthdays and sending holiday cards to your new husband's family?*

In the past society automatically assumed this was a wife's responsibility. Happily, times have changed, and today there's no set rule. You can handle card-writing and gift-giving any way that works for you as a couple. Some women enjoy shopping; others resent the assumption that they're responsible for remembering their spouse's old college buddies or distant relatives the minute they're married. The most important thing is to talk the issue over and come to an agreement on how you're going to handle it. You might want to buy a birthday book to help you keep track of important dates, or enter the dates into the scheduling program on your personal computer. If your husband doesn't know his relatives' or close friends' birthdays or anniversary dates, ask his mother or a sibling, and the friends themselves. Refer to the book at the beginning of each month to see whose birthdays are coming up, then pick a day to shop together or to brainstorm about what people might need. I like to keep a dozen or so birthday cards on hand at all times, just in case of "emergencies." Next time you're at a good card shop, pick up a few extra cards to have in reserve. Choose an assortment to include cards for anniversaries, weddings, condolence, baby birth, congratulations, and birthday. A couple of additional blank cards will ensure you have all eventualities covered.

Chapter 12

Life as Mr. and Mrs.

Let's Get Organized

The honeymoon is over! It's back to reality time. Now you're ready to get down to the business of starting your life with your new husband.

Frequently at the beginning of a marriage some things can go wrong. Even if you've lived together for several years, marriage tends to change our expectations and even our behavior. The early months of married life are an ideal opportunity to mend little problems and develop effective ways of resolving your differences so that the problems won't crop up again and again. I always compare small problems in a relationship to cracks in concrete. The cracks at first might seem insignificant, but if they're not mended, they can spread to become rifts and eventually crevasses.

Early on you'll have many issues to discuss. For example, who's going to pay for what? How will you pool your finances? Who will make sure the bills are paid on time? Who will do the cooking? Who's going to take care of the housecleaning? If you can afford to have domestic help, who will show the person what to do and take responsibility for paying her or him?

First, figure out how your home should run. Perhaps you're a pack rat and your husband is a compulsive neatnik. Maybe you're used to having your own apartment and prefer to keep separate his-and-her cabinets for toiletries, while your husband comes from a large family and is used to a more communal living style where everyone's personal items share space on the bathroom shelves. It's a good idea to sit down and discuss how you're going to manage the house, who's going to be responsible for cleaning, and how neat and tidy you expect each other to keep things.

If you both have busy schedules and demanding careers, each of you should share the household chores. You might want to make a list of those chores and the amount of time each takes on a weekly basis, to help divide the work equally. Then plan on setting aside a few hours on a weekend afternoon or one night a week where the two of you can do the chores together. Or if you both work long hours and can afford domestic help, you might consider hiring a maid to come in and help, if not on a daily basis, then once or twice a week to do the heavy cleaning and laundry.

A Functional Home

In my opinion it is much easier to be organized than disorganized. I find that the more I keep my home in order, the easier it is for me to get things done quickly and efficiently. Here are a few hints that have helped me and that might work for you, too:

Handling Maid Service or Domestic Help

With today's busy lifestyles, many of us find it helpful to pay someone to clean house once or twice a month. A fortunate few have part-time or even full-time household help. But conflicts often arise over expectations and performance. I frequently hear friends complain that the person they've hired to help with housekeeping never does what she (or he) is supposed to do. Usually when this happens, it's not because the help is lazy or inept; it's because the people doing the hiring haven't explained what they want. In the corporate world, employees are given verbal or written job descriptions and alerted to company policies, rules, restrictions, and so on. It should be no different in your home. In addition to making sure the maid or housekeeper understands what the working hours and remuneration will be, you might make a written list of the tasks you want completed. If you're not satisfied with something, tell the cleaning person politely that there's a small problem. Then show him or her what's wrong specifically and explain what you expect next time. Just as every corporate job comes with incentives, make sure you create incentives for those who help regularly in your house. Every year I send my maid on a vacation to her native country with the plane ticket paid for by my frequent-flyer mileage. This doesn't cost me anything and goes a very long way in ensuring a positive, helpful attitude on her part. A cash bonus over the holidays will show your cleaning person how important he or she is to your household. If you don't feel comfortable giving cash, you could get your domestic worker a gift certificate at a nice restaurant, a department store, or a beauty salon for a facial or massage.

• Keep a list of items that you want to have in the refrigerator or kitchen cabinet at all times. (I have prepared a sample list of "Ten Indispensable Items to Keep on Hand" in the chapter on entertaining.)

• Shop for groceries on a regular basis so that you'll be able to pull a lunch or dinner together at a moment's notice for yourselves or guests. Even if you're returning from out of town, if you have a grocer who will deliver, you can fax a list of items to your grocer and have them sent over so you don't return to an empty larder.

• Keep "public" spaces, such as living and dining rooms, clean and neat at all times so that you can receive unexpected guests or entertain at a moment's notice should the opportunity arise. If a neighbor drops by, you won't want to keep him or her standing in the hallway or on the front porch because you're too embarrassed to let anyone in.

• As a safety valve, it's fine to keep one "mess room," maybe a den or a library, where you can put your feet up and have piles of books and newspapers spread around.

• Keep your clothes neat and tidy. As soon as a few shirts start to pile up on the back of a chair, it gets easier to add to the pile. Before you know it, you'll have a mess.

• Establish a place that will function as your home office. Here you'll likely have a filing cabinet and a desk where you can write checks, keep personalized stationery, stamps, address book, scissors, tape, receipts, records of paid bills, a ledger, and so on.

• Establish a place where the tool kit will be kept so that you'll be able to find it easily. The basic tool kit should have a hammer, screwdriver, picture-hanging wire and nails, tape measure, and so on. Do the same with a mending/sewing kit and a shoe-cleaning kit. I often go to dime stores and find wonderful hold-everything plastic containers with compartments that help me organize small items like buttons or nails. It's also a great idea to take larger plastic containers and label them for shoe-polishing, tools, picture-hanging, computer cords and attachments, mending and sewing, or whatever else you need and use.

Often with couples one partner is the neatnik and the other is more casual about housekeeping. It's important for each partner to be considerate of the other's standards. If you are the neat one, don't nag your husband endlessly. Try to find ways to motivate him to pick up after himself, and make sure there is at least one area around the house that he doesn't have to worry about keeping neat as a pin. If your husband is the clean freak, remember that it bothers him to have a messy home, and work on developing neater habits. When your home is in order, it creates a sanctuary where you can relax and recharge your mental batteries. A messy living space, on the other hand, wastes your time and can make you feel stressed and unhappy.

Your home certainly doesn't have to look like the displays at a department store. On the contrary, a stiff, formal home can be as uncomfortable as a messy one. The idea is to make sure your home is set up for living and enjoyment. Furniture was designed to be used, not saved for special occasions like Victorian parlors.

Everyday Etiquette

As someone who comes into contact with many people on a regular basis, especially brides and grooms planning their weddings, I am constantly observing people's interactions in social settings. Although I have no desire to become the next Emily Post, here are a few thoughts on behaving with social grace and poise. These are things I always notice—admiring the gracious, chuckling at the humorous, and cringing at the just plain horrifying.

• Avoid applying lipstick, powdering your nose, or brushing your hair at the dinner table. Personal grooming takes place in the ladies' room or before leaving home.

• If a man makes an effort to be a gentleman by holding a door open for you or by standing up when you enter a room or approach a table, say thank you or at the very least nod an acknowledgment. Considering oneself liberated is never an excuse to be rude. Men don't make these gestures to be sexist; they're simply being polite.

• Watch the messages your wardrobe and makeup are sending. Less is more, when it comes to elegance in jewelry and makeup. People tend to hold on to first impressions of the way you look, so make sure your look is right the first time.

• Make an effort to be polite and charming with your spouse's friends and business associates. Of course, he should do the same for you. In a very real sense you are each other's ambassadors to the outside world. Not only will making a good impression expand your circle of friends, but you can often help your spouse get ahead in his career and vice versa. There's no need to be phony; simply be yourself, don't be pretentious, and make an effort to be friendly and to put others at ease. For example, whenever I notice someone standing alone at a cocktail party, I always approach the person and introduce myself. Ninety-nine times out of hundred, they are delighted to have someone to talk to, while I make a new friend and enjoy an interesting conversation.

• Chewing gum doesn't belong at lunches or parties. It's hard to talk when you're chewing, and it detracts from the appearance of a confident, sophisticated married woman. If you've got to have something, carry breath mints in your purse.

• Watch your language. Thanks to cable TV and movies, most of us have become so accustomed to profanity that we hardly notice it slipping into our vocabulary now and then. But fight the temptation to swear. It always leaves a bad impression. (If you're all alone and a hammer falls on your foot, be my guest. You might as well get it out of your system.)

• Don't drink too much alcohol in public. Limit yourself to a glass of wine or two with dinner or a cocktail or two at a party. Know your limits, and pace yourself. You wouldn't want to end up crying in the ladies' room at a dinner party or pouring your heart out to one of your business associates and becoming the subject of office gossip after the Christmas party. Also, beware of the truth-serum effect that liquor can have. With a little liquid courage, you just might blurt out something you'll regret. Even if you *can* hold your liquor, you won't make a very good impression on your (or your husband's) business associates by matching them scotch for scotch.

• Don't hang on your husband. Everyone knows you're married; there's no reason to coo sweet nothings to him, give him a neck massage, kiss him fondly, engage in childlike talk, or blow in his ear in front of friends. It's immature, and it makes everyone else uncomfortable.

• Avoid gossip. I was always told as a child, "If you can't say something nice, don't say anything at all." If someone starts to tell me a negative tale about a mutual friend or to gripe about their spouse, I politely tell them that I don't feel

What's in a Name: Changing Your ID

If you've decided to hyphenate or take your husband's last name, be sure to change your business cards, checkbook, credit cards, and identification as soon as possible to avoid confusion. Always make sure your passport is up to date in case an unexpected trip comes up and you need or want to travel immediately.

If you've moved into a new home together, especially if it's in a new city, fill out a forwarding address form from the post office. Send notices of your change in address to anyone you receive mail from regularly, especially credit card companies, banks that send you monthly balance statements, magazine and newspaper subscriptions, and so on.

Alternatively, print change-of-address cards using attractive stationery, creative computer graphics and fonts, and possibly a scanned photo of your new home to send to friends. (If you don't have a scanner, copy shops will often scan photos for a minimal charge or perhaps you can borrow a scanner at work after hours.) The change-of-address card should contain your current pertinent information, including new address, phone and fax numbers, and your e-mail address.

I also suggest you order personalized stationery and a set of mailing labels with your new name or with both of your names on them. You can order personalized items through mail-order catalogs inexpensively.

A Word on Relocating

Though moving to a new city can be exciting,

many newlyweds also find it traumatic. You've distanced yourself from your old comfortable network of friends. You've lost your favorite restaurants and shops. You've even lost the familiar route that you took to work every morning and knew so well that you could drive it with your eyes closed.

Of course, you'll make wonderful new friends together, you'll discover great new restaurants and shops, and you'll likely find an exciting new job if you don't already have one. In the meantime, however, the days can seem long and lonely. It's often particularly hard for a wife who has moved to a city where her husband was already living and had long since established a routine and a circle of friends. Although only time will make the new city feel like home, here are a few hints to make the transition more pleasant.

• Throw a dinner party for your husband's colleagues and their significant others. Have fun using your new china, cooking appliances, serving pieces, and other wedding gifts. Chances are you'll soon become part of their circle of wives and girlfriends or at least make one or two new friends who will invite you to lunches, or to join them in aerobics classes, book clubs, and so on.

• Set aside a certain amount of time every week to explore the city together as a couple. Even if your husband already knows his way around and is eager to introduce you to his favorite hot spots, make an effort to find new places. They'll feel extra special if you've discovered them together.

• Research clubs and groups that pique your interests, whether it's joining a gym and striking up a conversation with the people in your yoga

comfortable discussing this topic. I might say, "You know, I'm sorry to hear that you're having problems with Susan. But you're both very dear friends of mine and I just don't feel comfortable getting into the middle of things." Then I change the subject. "I've been meaning to ask you, how are the plans for your new house coming?" Or "So tell me, how is work going for you? Did you finish the project you mentioned last week?" If that doesn't work, I might suggest going to refill drinks or checking out the view from another room. A change of scenery sometimes gets the person's mind off the gossip. And if that doesn't work, I politely excuse myself and find someone with more pleasant conversation to make rather than enabling their bad habits. Gossip is a very damaging habit. Most important, if a trusted friend tells you something in confidence, never discuss it with anyone else. You should never violate someone's trust; you could lose a friend or tarnish a valuable relationship.

• Steer clear of family politics. If your husband doesn't speak to his father, I'd recommend that you be polite and cordial. However, don't try to mend fences or call a family summit to end the cold war. His family dynamics were ingrained over many years before you arrived on the scene, so chances are you won't be able to correct them. What's more, it's important to respect your husband's feelings and to avoid putting him into a situation where he would feel uncomfortable. Naturally, the same applies to his relationship with your family. By always being cordial and gracious, you are leaving the opportunity open for reconciliation.

• If someone thinks enough of you to invite you to a party or dinner, RSVP promptly, and unless a true emergency arises, don't cancel. People who entertain have spent a lot of time and effort to create a special gathering for their friends or business associates. There's nothing worse than having friends find out you gave them a trumped-up excuse for missing their party because you weren't in the mood or wanted to attend a better event.

• Be punctual for social as well as business events. If you're running late, call. There's a phone booth on practically every corner of every street in every city in the country, so when someone says she couldn't find a phone, everyone knows it's a poor excuse.

• Become a good listener. Pay attention to people's names when you're introduced. You might need to introduce that person to someone else a few minutes later, and it's embarrassing and insulting to say, "I apologize; I have forgotten your name." I am terribly guilty of this! Ask others about themselves, find mutual points of interest, and contribute to the conversation, but don't pontificate. If you do forget someone's name, apologize and make an effort to remember it for the future.

• Don't argue with your spouse, criticize him, correct him, or belittle him in front of other people. (Ideally, don't do it in private, either.) And don't pout if you're angry with him.

• Watch your tone of voice. It's not what you say but how you say it. Be gracious if you send your steak back to the chef because it's underdone.

• Eat and drink as quietly and politely as possible. We've all experienced losing our appetites listening to someone slurp his soup or gulp down her drink.

class or volunteering at the local Humane Society. You might do some of these on your own and some as a couple. Your husband may feel that he's already got all the friends he needs, but remind him that you don't want to become an extension of his life; you want to establish a new life together and a life of your own.

• Make an effort to keep in touch with friends from home. Thanks to e-mail, talk is less costly than ever. And if you prefer to chat on the phone, go ahead. It's worth the higher phone bills if it makes you feel happier. My family lives on another continent, and I never think twice about picking up the phone and chatting with them. Family and friendships need to be nurtured and cared for just as romantic relationships do.

• Invite friends from home to come visit, and plan to go back and visit them when you can. That way you can merge your old life with your new one.

• Make a list of things that make you happy. These can be songs that lift your spirits, colors that cheer you up, comfort foods, hobbies, or games and physical activities you enjoy. Keep your list handy, and pick an item every time you feel down in the dumps. For example, if you love gardening, go out and buy a half-dozen bright red geraniums and plant them in a window box to cheer up your new home. Take a brisk walk listening to a favorite tape to help create pleasant associations with your new neighborhood. Or to lift both your own spirits and your husband's, you might recreate your first date by ordering Indian food, opening a bottle of wine, and renting a video of the first movie you ever saw together.

• Share your feelings with each other. If he's

content in the new city, he may not even notice that the transition is tough for you. If you want your marriage to succeed, you'll need to learn to communicate your concerns and be supportive of each other.

• Keep an open mind. Try not to judge the new place too harshly or quickly or make constant comparisons between it and your old home. Think of it as a move forward.

• Finally, give yourself time. It's natural to feel a little homesick and blue for the first few months in a new place. But by keeping busy and getting involved, you'll quickly find yourself beginning to adjust.

• If someone makes a thoughtful gesture for you, be appreciative and acknowledge it graciously. Never expect gifts, compliments, or favors. This holds true for the little things your husband does for you. If he cleans your car or stops to pick up your dry cleaning, let him know how much you appreciate his thoughtfulness.

• Remember that the generally accepted etiquette guidelines when dining out hold that the person who does the inviting handles payment. If someone asks you to lunch or dinner and tells you they've made reservations, you should assume that they plan to pay. If, on the other hand, the invitation is more casual, such as "Why don't we meet for lunch next week?" chances are they may expect to split the bill.

Chapter 13

Money Matters

Sorting Out Your Finances and Planning for the Future

As you planned your wedding, you learned to start thinking as a couple. Whether you were choosing who was going to be included in your wedding party, what to serve your guests for dinner, or where to spend your honeymoon, it was (hopefully) a joint decision that you both found acceptable. Now it's time to start thinking as a couple in terms of finances.

You'll face some big responsibilities in life now that you're married. You'll need to take care of health insurance, life insurance, auto insurance, insurance for your home and possessions, and all sorts of other things. You'll need to make sure that you have a savings account to cover unexpected expenses and to have a nest egg for the future. You'll probably want to start saving to buy a home, a car, new furniture, and other major items to get started in your life together. You might even have funds that were given to you as wedding presents that you'll need to invest or use to cover the new expenses of married life.

Just as you planned and discussed the details of your wedding carefully and meticulously to make it a success, you'll want to plan your financial future together. You wouldn't want to get yourselves into debt, and you certainly wouldn't want arguments over money to upset your marriage. That's why it's very important that from day one you decide what's going to happen with regard to finances, who's going to contribute what, and how it's going to be divvied up and spent at the end of the day.

Yours, Mine, and Ours

One of the first steps toward sorting out your finances and planning your future together is pooling your monetary resources. Of course, there's no law dictating that everything the two of you own must become communal property. Thankfully we're long past the days of dowries and chattel, when women and all their possessions were handed over to their husbands as soon as they said "I do." However, at the very least you should put part of your earnings into a joint bank account. After all, trust is the most important aspect of marriage, and it should extend to every part of your relationship, from fidelity to honesty about your earnings. Pooling your financial resources is an excellent way to help build trust.

Even before you actually tie the knot, it's a good idea to sit down and have a heart-to-heart talk about how you're going to handle your finances. It might not sound like as much fun as sitting down to pick a china pattern or a honeymoon destination, but it's simply part of taking a practical, responsible approach toward life. Start by asking yourselves these questions:

What are our combined monthly earnings?

What amount do we both have in savings, stocks, bonds, and so on?

What types of accounts are we going to open and where?

What are we going to do with our joint finances?

Are there major purchases we want to start saving for or to buy immediately?

What are our long-term goals, and what will it cost us to reach them?

How much do we need to start saving now to reach the goals we've set for ourselves?

What monthly expenses do we have (food, rent, clothing, and the like)? Don't forget about outstanding debts such as school loans and credit card balances.

Once you've answered these questions, you'll be able to create a practical budget for yourselves. Determine where you can afford to live, what kind of car you can afford to drive, how you can afford to entertain, how you can afford to dress, what vacations you can afford to take this year, and so on.

It's also an excellent idea to find an accountant or, if you already work with someone you trust, make an appointment to meet with that person to discuss how your tax situation will change now that you're married, and how buying a house or apartment will affect your deductions.

Another option is to find a financial planner to help you invest as a couple. Just as you carefully researched vendors for your wedding, be sure to get personal referrals from trusted friends or family members before discussing your finances with an outsider. It's a good idea to read up on this topic and to review the fine print before signing any documents. In the same way that certain wedding consultants will push you toward florists or caterers who give them a commission, unscrupulous financial planners may steer you toward investments that do not correspond to your personal goals.

Since you've decided that you're going to live the rest of your lives together, you'll need to make some plans for the long-term financial future. For example, you might want to purchase life insurance now since it's much cheaper to buy when you're young. The longer you wait, the more it will cost. You might also want to discuss what types of retirement accounts or pension plans you both have through your employers and independently to determine if these plans will meet your retirement needs or if you need to supplement them.

Establish the parameters of how to handle your money, and make sure you're both comfortable with the arrangements. Be honest about any reservations you have. It's better to bring up your worries now than to panic later when the bills come in. If, for example, you know that the austere savings plan you've devised will cause a hardship at work when your coworkers head out to a collegial lunch and you're stuck brown-bagging it at your desk, revise the plan. Be realistic and build some enjoyment into your lives. No matter how much you need to buy that five-bedroom Colonial home in two years, making yourselves unhappy in the meantime will put undue stress on your marriage. By the time you can afford that house, you may not even want to live in it together!

Once you've developed a workable budget and savings plan, assign one person to be responsible for the finances. That person will make sure that all the bills are paid on time, that the checkbook stays up to date, that receipts for taxes are stashed in one convenient place, and so on. In essence, he or she becomes the family bookkeeper/accountant.

However, this doesn't mean that he or she becomes the keeper of the purse strings. I'm certainly not advocating a setup where you have to approach your husband and beg for an allowance every time you want to buy a dress. Just the opposite is true. Every budget should include a certain amount of fun, disposable income—whether it's $50, $500, or $5,000—that each of you can spend per month. Figuring this out is a joint decision. After you've settled on the amount, you'll both have a clear understanding of how often you can take friends to lunch, shop, and so on. It's up to each of you to be responsible and stick to the limits you've set.

Keep the lines of communication open. The person overseeing the financials will need to make sure the other person understands the reality of your monetary situation. "Yes, we can afford to go to Bali for two weeks, first class all the way this year." Or, "No, we just bought a house. So we're going to spend a week at Dad's cabin for our vacation this summer."

Resolving Money Conflicts

If you both come from similar financial backgrounds, discussing money may come easily. However, for many couples it's a source of considerable tension. A survey conducted by Miriam Arond and Samuel L. Pauker, M.D., for their book, *The First Year of Marriage*, suggested that money is the leading source of arguments among newlyweds. It also showed that more than half of all newlyweds experience marital problems stemming from money. Still other surveys indicate that money conflicts are the most common reason couples file for divorce.

So is money really "the root of all evil" when it comes to marriage? In my experience, most often it is not the actual money that's causing the problem. Miscommunication and misunderstanding about issues surrounding money are usually the real culprits. That's because money means a great many different things to different people. Perhaps you tend to be very conservative financially because you developed your spending and saving habits while you were struggling at work to put yourself through college. Your husband, on the other hand, might have parents who paid for his tuition and raised him to see spending freely on lavish trips and gifts for friends as the best way to enjoy life. If you have parents or grandparents who lived through the Depression, chances are that saving money gives them a sense of safety and security. They probably see spending extravagantly as dangerous and foolish. By contrast, those of us raised in more affluent times often associate spending with freedom, independence, and success.

Chances are you've already learned quite a bit about your husband's views on money from dating him and planning a wedding together. However, it's often very helpful to sit down and discuss not only the practical issues mentioned above but the emotional connotations money holds for each of you. How did your family perceive money? Who was responsible for making sure the bills were paid on time? If your father handled all the finances and hid the credit cards from your mother who was a profligate spender, it might seem strange to you to become the family bookkeeper now. Conversely, if you've been living on your own and paying your bills for the past ten years, you might resent your husband expecting you to suddenly hand your paycheck over to him every two weeks.

Trust me, there's nothing worse than arguing over money. And the simplest way to avoid it is to keep an open mind and open lines of communication. Try to understand each other's opinions and ideas about money. If you're used to spending only a few dollars every morning for a bagel, don't condemn your husband for wanting to enjoy a champagne brunch now and then. Remember, neither of you is right or wrong; you just have different opinions. Marriage is about compromising and finding a new path together. Figure out how many champagne brunches and how many bagels your budget allows; then plan to enjoy a certain number of each together. Once you quell your fears of overspending, you might discover that you enjoy an elegant brunch after all. Likewise, your husband might find that savoring fresh bagels, smoked salmon, and juice together on your patio is more romantic than dining out. Particularly if you add a fresh flower in a crystal vase, set the table with linen napkins and a silver ice bucket, and make mimosas with sparkling wine and freshly squeezed orange juice!

It's a good idea to start out a marriage with a budget that you have both agreed upon. Set aside some time, say, on a Saturday morning, and list the items that need to be covered. Then work out the budgeted amounts for each item. Be sure to include "savings" as a budgeted item, as well as any payments on debt, such as credit cards, school loans, or car payments. Also include savings for items you are planning for, such as a vacation or a down payment on a home. Designate one person to handle the checkbook, and monitor the budget a couple of times a month. If you stick to your budget, you'll be in much better financial shape, and you'll have more money for the things that really matter to you.

Having opposing views on money is not necessarily a recipe for disaster. Perhaps you can help him learn to loosen up and get over his guilt at spending his hard-earned money on activities or items he genuinely enjoys. Perhaps he can help you adopt a more practical, responsible approach to managing your credit cards. There's nothing wrong with keeping some funds separate for miscellaneous items, as long as you both agree on the amounts. If he starts to hyperventilate every time he sees you look longingly at a department store, and you think he's "wasting" your disposable income at the driving range, you might solve it by pooling a portion of your monthly earnings into a joint fund for groceries, rent, and so on. Then keep a separate account for your "fun" purchases, such as his golf outings or your accessories.

There is lots of information available to help a couple who are merging their finances and just starting out on married life. In addition to books on the subject, there are personal finance software programs and a myriad of on-line informational resources. Also, take a look at on-line banking and on-line investing services, which can save time and money.

Chapter 14

Effortless Elegance: An Introduction to Entertaining

I t always amazes me how many brides and grooms move into their new homes, unpack all their china, silver, and crystal, admire it briefly as they write their thank-you notes...and then pack it away again. All those beautiful items from their wedding registry disappear into the china cabinet to collect dust!

Some of the most valuable advice I can give you as a bride is very simple: Make every occasion a special one. Why should Christmas Eve be any more important than a romantic Saturday night dinner with your husband? Why not enjoy Sunday brunch with your best china, even if you risk chipping a piece? There's no reason to own fine things unless you're really going to use them and bring them to life.

Entertaining not only gives you the opportunity to enjoy your home and favorite furnishings, it's a great way to spend quality time with your husband and mutual friends. When I entertain, I *always* use my good dishes. I once lived through an earthquake and I lost some very valuable items. Looking back, I wish only that I had used them and enjoyed them on a day-to-day basis. China and silver are meant to be used, not closeted away. The more you use them, the better they look.

Basically there are three reasons why people don't entertain.

First, they're afraid it will cost too much.

Second, they think it will take too much time.

And third, they don't believe they have the ability.

Let's deal with these issues. A good meal is not necessarily made from expensive and hard-to-find ingredients. If you're new at entertaining, start simply. Don't begin with a four-course meal for eight that requires ten steps of preparation for each ingredient and a map of the city to find them all. Some of the most enjoyable evenings I've spent with friends were when I just roasted a chicken, steamed asparagus at the last minute, prepared a quick salad, and set a beautiful table.

Finally eliminate your anxiety about entertaining. Don't let gourmet cookbooks and lavish decorating magazines scare you off. Entertaining isn't about impressing people; it's about having fun. Remember the first time you sat down in front of a computer? Chances are you were hopelessly intimidated. However, today you and the computer are probably almost joined at the hip. Keep your entertaining very simple until you begin to master the techniques of the kitchen and the dinner table. You'll build confidence as you go. The point is to make entertaining part of your day-to-day life so that you feel comfortable with it, instead of viewing it as a huge, monumental affair each time you decide to invite someone over.

Refining Your Sense of Style

The first step toward entertaining as a married couple is for both of you to discover your personal sense of style. Are you extremely casual, informal, very formal, or somewhere in between? Few people entertain formally today unless it's for a fiftieth wedding anniversary or a visiting head of state. And since heads of state don't visit too often, start with fun rather than formal. To define your sense of style, ask yourself a few questions.

• What types of items did you register for: Elegant, formal place settings? Or simple, casual settings? Traditional or contemporary? Subdued or bright and bold?

• What types of events do you enjoy–more casual or formal?

• Do you prefer impromptu outings or elaborately planned ones?

• Which do you enjoy more on a weekend: Getting dressed up for a sophisticated candlelit dinner followed by an evening at the theater? Or a casual backyard barbecue followed by an afternoon at a baseball game? Perhaps you like both, depending on your mood. Keep in mind that formality and elegance don't have to be part of the same sentence. It's easy to plan a chic, elegant affair with a casual ambience and attitude–it just depends on how you set the table, what you serve, and how you structure the evening. I love to set a beautiful table, but even though it looks elegant, I always keep the atmosphere fun and casual and ensure the guests are comfortable by making them feel very welcome.

• Think about parties and dinners you've attended at friends' houses. Which were your favorites? Which made you want to stay all evening, and which made you want to bolt for the door? What types of party themes have you found charming? Which made you cringe?

• What size gatherings make you feel most comfortable?

• What are your favorite types of restaurants and clubs? Lively and crowded? Quiet and refined? Exotic and ethnic or homey and all-American? What types of foods and cocktails do you enjoy?

Your answers should give you some good clues as to what types of entertaining you'll enjoy as a couple and which you'll feel most comfortable hosting. You might want to jot down four or five ideas for dinners or informal parties to host over the next few months, based on what you and your husband discover from the questions above.

Who Does What

Next you'll need to decide who will handle what aspect of the party planning. Determine as a couple who's going to take on what entertaining skills, be they cooking, ordering the take-out, preparing the house, setting the table, selecting the wine, or washing the dishes. Chances are each of you will enjoy and excel at different aspects of entertaining. Among my friends some of the men are fabulous chefs, while their wives are totally into wine. Other female friends set beautiful tables, while their husbands are terrific hosts who can make anyone feel at home instantly.

Decide whose role is whose, based on what you both like and dislike. No matter how capable you are as a hostess, don't let all the responsibilities land in your lap. Even if you love parties, you won't enjoy struggling over four dozen canapés while your husband is on the golf course or lounging in front of the TV. You both have a social responsibility to entertain. Besides, it's much more fun when you do it together. Just think of it as another way to bond as a couple and to learn those important negotiating and compromising skills. You have your home and all your beautiful things; you have your mutual friends; there's no better way of bringing it all together than entertaining!

When you're planning your next party, set aside an evening after work when neither of you is too worn out or preoccupied. Then sit down over a cocktail and hash out the details:

- What's the theme going to be (if there is one)?
- Who are we going to invite?
- What are we going to serve?
- What are we going to spend?
- Who's going to be responsible for what?

If the planning starts to become a chore, stop. Rethink the event and come up with an idea that sounds more fun and has more of a twist to it. Or postpone your conversation until you're both in the mood to talk about the party.

Getting Started

We live in a society of casual Fridays, relaxed-fit jeans, and comfort foods. So take that trend to heart in your entertaining. The simplest gatherings are often the most fun. I sometimes invite a few friends over on the spur of the moment, then drop by the fish market on my way home and pick up a few dozen shrimp, some cocktail sauce, and a bottle of champagne. Or maybe a baguette of bread, some cheese, and a bottle of red wine. Either option makes a wonderful appetizer that you can serve before going out for the evening.

When entertaining, you need to have a formula. Stick to menus that allow you to do most, if not all, of the preparation in advance so that you can be a guest at your own party. You should be glued to your chair, not chained to the stove! It's no fun spending the entire evening in the kitchen while your guests are laughing and talking in the living room. All too soon they will have gone, and all you'll have to look forward to is a huge pile of dishes.

Or skip the cooking altogether. You get no medals for picking 153 perfectly ripened cherries from the tree and painstakingly baking a pie from scratch. In fact, great take-out can be your best ally. Order a variety of appetizers or dishes from one of your favorite ethnic restaurants, then transfer the food from its flimsy cardboard cartons to your serving pieces. Or drop one of your good casserole dishes off at your favorite local restaurant and have them prepare an entree in it for you to pick up the

The "Indispensables"–

Things to Keep on Hand at All Times

1. The basics: milk, butter, eggs, flour, sugar, and a selection of spices
2. A good vinaigrette salad dressing
3. Frozen chicken, veal, or vegetable stock
4. Dijon mustard
5. Prewashed salad
6. Dried pasta and rice
7. Canned Italian tomatoes
8. Good-quality virgin olive oil
9. A selection of interesting vinegars, including red wine and balsamic
10. A bottle of good vodka in the freezer, several bottles of chilled white wine, one bottle of champagne, and plenty of ice

following day. Leave the food preparation to the experts, and concentrate on something you enjoy. If you like decorating more than cooking, have fun setting a beautiful table and making your home warm and inviting. Before the party, find a great new set of vintage dessert plates to serve that fabulous store-bought cake on. Or buy dozens of candles, both plain and scented, as well as new hand towels for the bathroom. Focus on whatever aspect of entertaining you enjoy most. You don't have to conform to anyone else's idea of "proper entertaining." The point is to make it appear effortless and to have fun at the same time.

Effortless Entertaining Ideas

Here are a few of my favorite formulas for casual entertaining. They're easy to put together and a lot of fun for both you and your guests. I hope you'll be inspired to try one or two. Or perhaps they'll trigger creative ideas of your own.

• Before going out to a show, invite a few friends over for cocktails and some simple but tasty appetizers, such as a loaf of crusty French bread and a few fabulous imported cheeses, toasted and spiced nuts, and marinated olives, or a few other fun and interesting items you find at a local gourmet shop, such as a pâté or fresh-smoked salmon. Another possibility: Grill a variety of interesting sausages, cut them into bite-size pieces, and serve them with one or two interesting sweet and spicy mustards. Don't forget toothpicks for dipping.

• After a show or an evening out with friends, invite them over for late-night coffee and dessert, such as a fresh fruit tart from a local bakery or a decadent chocolate cake you baked earlier in the day. Serve this with fresh-brewed coffee, a dessert wine, or cognac and good cigars.

• Host a wine-tasting party. I've done this on many occasions, and besides having a lot of fun, my friends and I have learned a great deal about particular types of wine. You'll want to include dinner or substantial hors d'oeuvres to keep your guests from drinking too much on an empty stomach. If you're serving red meat, purchase four or five different bottles of cabernet or merlot; for poultry you might try a zinfandel tasting, and for seafood several French Chablis or Rieslings from Alsace.

• You can use the same tasting-party concept with any type of food or drink you and your friends want to learn more about. Get each of your guests to bring a different brand of smoked salmon or caviar. Or host a scotch- or vodka-tasting party. Cover the labels of the bottles, and give everyone a few slips of paper and a pen for taking notes and grading the contents. Then compare everyone's thoughts. Jot down the names of the types your guests like best so that you can serve them in the future. Always be sure to offer enough food to balance the alcohol, and create a menu where the food and beverage complement each other–such as caviar with champagne or vodka, smoked salmon with aquavit, meat with red wine, fish with white wine, cheese with port, desserts with dessert wine.

• Host an easy and informal afternoon barbecue or a clambake. Even men who won't touch a casserole dish with a ten-foot pole are often masters at grilling steaks and steaming lobsters. He can barbecue while you prepare a few salads, sauces, and baked potatoes. Make the table interesting by using small, colorful linen dish towels instead of napkins.

• Host a seafood potluck. Have one person bring lobster, one bring oysters, and another bring shrimp. Just make sure you don't choose anyone who's notoriously late to bring the appetizers.

• Invite friends over for a lazy Sunday morning brunch when you have leisure time on your hands and no particular agenda. It doesn't take a rocket scientist to scramble some eggs, bake or buy muffins, brew a good pot of coffee, and squeeze some juice. Rather than the traditional orange or grapefruit juice, try an unusual combination like raspberry and cranberry, or make smoothies with strawberries, papaya, yogurt, and ice.

• Afternoon tea is another of my favorite easy and elegant ways to host a party. All that's required is an assortment of fine teas, a few colorful garnishes such as lemon and orange slices and cinnamon sticks, perhaps a selection of English-style finger sandwiches (small egg salad, tuna salad, and salmon-and-cream-cheese sandwiches with the crusts removed), pastries from your favorite bakery, and a batch of delicious, homemade cheese scones with whipped cream and jam.

• Decide to have a series of theme dinners with a group of friends. Each one of you can host what you do best. Somebody might prepare unbelievable barbecued ribs. Maybe somebody else makes a great paella or wonderful tamales.

• Buffet suppers work for both large and small gatherings, and they can be as casual or elegant as

When setting up a buffet, work from left to right. Start your buffet with the plates, flatware, and napkins. It's easy to wrap the flatware in the napkins, or the flatware can be placed on a tray or in a basket set beside the napkins. Next to it would be the bread, then the salad, cold dishes, and finally the hot food, and condiments at the end of the buffet. If you are serving a specific wine to compliment the menu you can also set out the wine and glasses to the right of the food for guests to help themselves.

Ideas for Making an Elegant Buffet Menu

• Avoid serving dishes that are swimming in sauce. Too much sauce will contaminate the flavor of all the other food items on the plate.

• Avoid placing seafood and meat dishes on the same buffet. They do not compliment one another. If you plan to serve both fish and meat, it is advisable to set up smaller stations and separate the foods.

• Limit your buffet to no more than five or six items, it reduces the time it takes for guests to be served and lessens the chances that the plate may becomes overloaded with too many foods.

• If you are hosting a large group of people, you might consider setting up more than one buffet. It will alleviate long lines for food. Alternatively, set up a variety of stations featuring different types of foods in order to provide your guests with choices.

* For a gastronomic experience pair the appropriate beverages to the food item, i.e., smoked salmon and Aquavit, caviar and Vodka, cheese and port, red wine and meat, white wine and fish, etc.

you desire. Prepare something simple like a savory summer casserole or lasagna, or order dinner for delivery. When serving a buffet, balance it by including a vegetable, a salad, a starch, and a protein. You can serve the salad before or after the main course. The buffet should always be set with items that complement each other. For example, I never serve fish, chicken, and red meat together on the same buffet table. If I am offering a selection of meats, chicken, and fish, I make a separate table for each, set with all the necessary complements. I always use lots of smaller plates rather than big ones, encouraging guests to take small portions and avoiding what I call the vulture syndrome.

Entertaining in a Restaurant

If you're not quite ready to invite a group of guests into your home for dinner, you might consider hosting a dinner party at a restaurant. As long as you stay organized, ensure that the restaurant staff understands what you want and expect from them, and agree on a bill you consider reasonable ahead of time, this can be a fun way to venture into the world of entertaining. Here are a few guidelines to keep in mind:

• Invite guests by phone or with a written invitation, depending on how formal you want the dinner to be or what restaurant you decide to use.

• Call the restaurant in advance to make the reservation. Call again the day of the dinner to reconfirm all the particulars. Chances are the person you will be speaking with is not the same person you spoke with before.

- Establish a single contact person at the restaurant.

- Select the wine, the menu, and–for larger groups–the seating with place cards in advance. Deliver or messenger the place cards to the restaurant along with a seating plan. Consider letting people choose their main courses and arranging a preset appetizer and dessert. If you don't know much about wine, buy a few wine books or consult a friend who loves wine for suggestions on what to order for a group. You might also ask the wine steward, manager, or maître d' for suggestions.

- If this is a special occasion, consider sending a floral centerpiece.

- Speak to the maître d' in advance to make sure wine and champagne will be chilled and at the table before you are seated.

- Call guests a few days ahead to make sure they know where the restaurant is and to let them know about any dress code restrictions.

- Fax your credit card number to the restaurant the day before the dinner with instructions to add the gratuity and fax a copy of the bill to you. That way you can avoid having the bill presented at the table.

Chapter 15

Becoming a Gracious Host

Setting the Stage

Now that you're ready to entertain, remember to appeal to all the senses. Often when we plan a party or dinner, we get so wrapped up in the cooking scenario that we forget about the ambience. Sight, smell, sound, and touch are just as important as taste. The tools of food, flowers, music, linens, and lighting can transform an ordinary setting into an extraordinary one.

For starters, invest in a few inexpensive dimmer switches and lots of candles. This gives you the opportunity to control the lighting in your home and create a cozy, intimate environment. It's also the most flattering and relaxing light for your guests since it makes everyone look better and younger. When people feel they look their best, they tend to be more relaxed and enjoy themselves more.

Music is the ultimate mood-maker. If you have a CD changer, program a variety of CDs for random play, so you won't have to worry about hopping up from the party constantly. Jazz, Latin, and other upbeat types of music work well for a cocktail hour. Switch to more subdued or classical background music during dinner. I like to play Billie Holiday, Sarah Vaughan, Shirley Horn, or light opera during dessert and coffee.

Be creative when decorating your table. We all think carefully about our personal appearance–what shoes, belts, and scarves to wear with which suits; how we wear our hair; what colors are most becoming to us. The same applies to the table. It's another opportunity to make a tasteful statement of personal style. Start with the basics–good china, silver, and crystal–then personalize it with unique accessories. I have a passion for browsing antique shops, scouring flea markets, shopping department stores, and perusing mail-order catalogs. I use all of these sources to collect special items for myself and for friends. I've found wonderful accent pieces that add just the right splash of color and rich texture for a stunning table. I also mix and match different china patterns and manufacturers to make the table interesting. For example, I pair crystal wineglasses with vintage champagne flutes and mix new dinner plates with antique salad plates. The more items to mix and match, the more dimension and character are added to the table.

Don't limit yourself to subdued, monochromatic settings. There's an almost limitless palette of colors, textures, shapes, and styles for the table. Spend some time thumbing through decorating magazines or browsing local home stores to stimulate your creativity.

It's fun to create interesting, unusual centerpieces as a focal point for your table. For a change of

A Starter Bar

A gracious hostess always keeps a well-stocked bar for guests' refreshment. The following is a list of the basic items the home bar should have. If you serve drinks often, you will want to augment this with other wine, spirits, or ingredients to make your specialties.

Equipment

Bottle opener

Champagne stopper

Citrus reamer

Corkscrew

Cocktail shaker with strainer

Ice bucket and ice tongs

Paring knife

Pitcher for water

Shot glass, jigger, or other measuring cup

Glassware

Old-fashioned glasses

Highball glasses

Martini glasses

Wine glasses

Water glasses

Champagne flutes

Brandy snifters*

Pilsner glasses*

*optional

Wine and Liquor

Blended whiskey

Brandy

Bourbon

Cognac

Gin

pace from cut and arranged fresh flowers, try using a piece of sculpture or a potted orchid surrounded by candles. A decorative bowl filled with lemons and limes or pomegranates and pears, or limes and coconuts or a variety of mixed fruits, can be just as colorful and interesting as flowers.

Collect whatever appeals to your personal sense of style–batik print tablecloths if you are into Thai cuisine, Venetian glass and silver with fine vintage linens if you prefer Northern Italian. Use your imagination to invent a table that oozes personality and that you can continually reinvent by using different colors and accessories.

Guess Who's Coming to Dinner: Creating an Interesting Guest List

People are often hesitant to expand their circle of friends and mix different groups from the office, from clubs, from the neighborhood, and so on. Why limit yourself and those you know? There are no rules that say you must invite all your friends from the office over together. They see one another all the time. Chances are they've exhausted most of their conversation in the elevator, on coffee breaks, and over lunch. They often resort to shop talk, leaving spouses and other "outsiders" excluded and bored.

Instead, consider inviting a few friends from the office with a couple from your book club and a friend who is visiting from out of town. It makes a much more dynamic and interesting gathering. Everyone gets to meet someone new, and unless your friends are all painfully shy, it will certainly stimulate lively conversation. In fact, when a friend introduces me to someone new, I make it a practice to invite my new acquaintance to a dinner party without our mutual contact.

I keep a journal on my computer noting whom I've invited with whom so that I'll remember to keep mixing new friends. I also try to jot down what I've served and how I set the table. That way I can glance back and recall what made for a particularly fun evening, and I avoid serving guests the same dish twice.

Whenever I invite more than six guests, I use place cards. This has nothing to do with formality; it just helps to balance the energy and avoid the awkwardness of trying to decide where to seat everyone once we are standing around the table. It's also another outlet for creatively decorating the table. You can handwrite the place cards, use a computer, or use a marker pen and write directly on a piece of fruit or gourd if it is in keeping with the look of your table.

I also make a point not to seat spouses next to each other. If I have two tables, I often put them at the different tables. I find they're less inhibited that way, and they feel freer to talk to others rather than to each other. Afterward the husbands and wives can tell each other about the interesting people they met and the stories they heard.

Don't be afraid to invite single friends, couples, and anyone else you think will enjoy the evening you're planning. Newlyweds often make the mistake of excluding single friends for fear they'll feel awkward around couples. On the contrary, the only time most of your single friends will feel awkward is when you suddenly start to leave them off the guest list. If you seat couples separately, singles won't feel like they're sitting on their own.

Rum

Scotch—one blended, one single malt

Tequila

Vodka

White (dry) and red (sweet) vermouth

White and red table wine of good quality (chardonnay or sauvignon blanc for the white and a Chianti classico, pinot noir, or zinfandel for the red)

Specialty Liquors, Liqueurs, and Wines

Campari

Cherry brandy

Cointreau orange liqueur

Crème de cassis (if you serve kirs)

Crème de cacao

Pernod or Ricard

Sambuca

Sherry (dry)

Mixers

Club soda

Soft drinks

Tonic water

Flavorings and Garnishes

Angostura bitters

Lemons

Limes

Maraschino cherries

Green olives

Sugar syrup or superfine sugar

Tabasco sauce

Worcestershire sauce

Here's one sample menu I often use:

Start by buying a prewashed salad, and toss in a few interesting extra ingredients such as toasted pine nuts, calamata olives, garlic croutons, or chunks of feta cheese. These add color, texture, and a savory Mediterranean taste.

Opt for a simple main course, such as salmon filets. Sprinkle them with coarse sea salt and pepper, sauté in a skillet over high heat for two minutes, then pop them into the oven in a glass baking dish for six minutes to complete the cooking while the guests are enjoying their salads. Serve the salmon on your best china surrounded by steamed fava or lima beans and cubed tomatoes, sprinkled with fresh basil and a generous drizzle of vinaigrette. Add a basket of warm, crusty sourdough bread or a rustic olive loaf from your best bread store.

For dessert, stop by or have your husband stop by a local bakery to pick up a fresh-baked tart, or serve fresh berries and sorbet with a shot of a favorite liqueur.

Think of your guest list as a recipe: Make sure there is always a bit of spice to liven up the table mix. It's fun to include the eccentric artist or adventurer to add flavor to the evening.

Doing the Right Thing: *What if friends ask if they can bring their child to my dinner party?*

Assuming you're planning an evening for adults, tell them their child is welcome to make himself or herself comfortable in the den or extra bedroom (provided you have room) and to please bring some videos and a game or two to keep the child entertained. Offer to order a pizza for the child if they wish, but explain that you've only invited adults and that you don't think the child–or the other adult guests–would feel very comfortable if he/she joined them for cocktails or dinner.

Making Guests Welcome

Before your guests arrive, take a few moments to glance around and make sure the stage is set: The candles are lit, the lights are dimmed, the music is playing, the wine is breathing, and you are relaxed and looking forward to a great evening. Open the door with a big smile. Take your guests' coats if they have any, and offer them a drink right away. Introduce the new arrivals to everyone, but not by saying, "This is James. He's the CEO of XYZ Corporation!" It sounds like you're trying to impress people or establish status. Instead say, "This is James, my friend from Ohio...from across the hall...from the office." Explain how you met or mention a mutual interest that the two you're introducing might have. "Mary, I'd like you to meet my friend James.

He just got back from two months in southern France. Mary's planning a trip to France next summer to study painting." Any topic you think might spark pleasant conversation makes a great introduction. During the course of dinner your friend's status as CEO of XYZ can come to light when the time is appropriate.

Be sure to engage everyone in conversation. There's always one person who wants the limelight, and it's up to you as the hostess to balance the energy of the table or the room. If someone hasn't gotten a word in edgewise, engage them in conversation. Ask them about themselves. Have they just been away? Are they planning a trip? What kind of new projects are they working on? Is their family well? What are they planning for their family during summer vacation this year? Are they going anywhere or staying at home to relax?

If you find there's a moment of silence at the dinner table, think of a subject that's making headlines right now to spark a new conversation. (One caveat: Avoid topics so controversial that discussing them might offend some of your guests or cause outright arguments such as politics or religion.) This is one reason it's very important to know what's going on in the world. Although you don't have to be ready for a guest spot on *Nightline*, it's important to read newspapers and magazines and to watch the news so you'll know something about current events. Small talk often revolves around them, and keeping up helps you function socially and boosts your confidence.

However, if someone's discussing a subject you're unfamiliar with, never feel ashamed to ask

Countdown to a Fabulous Party

12. Get organized. Tackle the preparation little by little. Don't leave everything for one frantic, last-minute planning marathon.

11. Make lists of everything you need to buy and do. Carry them with you, and revise or cross items off as you go.

10. Create an interesting guest list. Mix groups of friends and introduce new people. Keep a running list of who has and hasn't RSVP-ed so you'll know how many to set the table for and how much of each item to buy. If the event is approaching but you haven't heard from one of the guests you invited, call to find out whether he or she plans to attend.

9. Choose the menu. Keep it simple but tasteful. Decide what you'll serve and how many courses, including wines and desserts. I always like to include some hot and some cold dishes. Make a list of all the ingredients you need to buy and from where. Figure out how much time you need to prepare dishes and, based on that, when guests should arrive.

8. Map out the timing. It's the key to a good party. Keep in mind that forty-five minutes to an hour is ideal for cocktails before dinner.

7. Create a flow for cocktail parties. For larger parties, I design small vignettes of self-contained areas and tables where food will be placed along with small plates and appropriate beverages, and set them up a day in advance. This creates an easy flow of traffic and prevents your guests from having to wait in line or hover around a single buffet table.

6. Plan your table setting. Decide on which china and linens to be used. Make notes on what colors and types of flowers to buy. Set the table as far in advance as possible. Clean and polish your serving utensils a day or two before the party.

5. Use stick-on notes to remind yourself of where each dish will go. Set out serving plates, bowls, and platters ahead of time. Label them with the stick-on notes to avoid last-minute confusion and to ensure that you have enough dishes for each course.

4. Confirm take-out and delivery orders. If you plan to order out, find reliable sources and confirm precisely when dishes will be collected or delivered.

3. Prepare as much of the food as you can ahead of time. You can wash, slice, and dice most vegetables a day before the party if you seal them in air-tight plastic bags or containers.

2. Leave as few tasks as possible for the day of the party. Ideally, the day of the party, all you'll have to do is set out the food, pick up an item or two you've had a restaurant prepare, and enjoy putting together the finishing touches.

1. Set a deadline of an hour before the party to get everything ready. Use forty minutes or so to take a bath and get yourself ready at a leisurely pace. In the twenty minutes before your guests arrive, put out the ice, add the finishing touches to the table, and get the appetizers ready. Light the candles, adjust the lights, turn on the music, open the wine, pour yourself a drink, and take a few moments to glance over the room and make sure everything is in place.

them to explain. Start with a comment like, "Pardon my ignorance, but how does X work?" Or "I'm not too familiar with that topic. What have you been hearing lately about it?" It does not show that you're dumb; it shows that you're interested in the conversation. What's more, it gives the person you're talking to a chance to air his or her views while feeling knowledgeable about the topic.

Perhaps the most important key to keeping the evening lively and interesting is timing. A cocktail hour is exactly what it says: one hour, at most! My formula is forty-five minutes for cocktails, and the remaining fifteen minutes to have all the guests seated for dinner, all within an hour of the invitation time. Keep this time frame in mind when you're planning the menu. For instance, if you're inviting guests at 7:30 P.M. and it takes a half hour to cook the first course, the food goes into the oven fifteen minutes after they arrive (presumably, 7:45 P.M.). Everyone should be sitting down at the table at 8:15 P.M. and dinner should be served at roughly 8:20 P.M.

One final rule of thumb for couples: If your husband heads off to the kitchen to fix cocktails, try not to leave your guests alone at the table until he returns. By and large one of you should always stay in the room or at the table with your guests.

Cocktails, Anyone?

Instead of serving the same old boring drinks every time friends come over, welcome guests by offering them a vodka martini, a cosmopolitan, a champagne cocktail, a Singapore sling, or any other offbeat cocktail.(Skip the paper umbrellas and plastic monkeys.) I serve creative cocktails often, and it invariably jump-starts the party. People respond with delight–"Ooh, I haven't had one of those in a long time!"

It's thoughtful to also serve interesting non-acoholic drinks as well. Don't just fall back on the usual diet soft drinks or water–be creative. Some of my favorite nonalcoholic highballs include passion fruit or mango nectar topped up with club soda and a sprig of fresh mint; a splash of Rose's lime juice with club soda, fresh mint, and a wedge of lime; and half lemon-lime soda, half club soda, with a dash of Angostura bitters.

As hosts, keep in mind that whenever you serve alcoholic beverages, you are responsible for ensuring that your guests get home safely. If anyone has had too much to drink, by all means call a cab, drive them home yourself, or discreetly ask another guest who is in a condition to drive to give your mutual friend a lift. A fifteen-dollar taxi ride is much less costly than a ticket or the risk of an accident.

Last-Minute Dinner Parties Without Panic

One of the best reasons to entertain is no reason at all. And some of the best parties I've attended were arranged with little notice. It's an old cliché, but sometimes husbands really do call at the last minute to ask if they can bring a few friends from the office home for dinner. At other times you might both decide at the spur of the moment to ask friends over. The good news is that planning and hosting a dinner party can be amazingly simple.

Ten Tips for Making Guests Feel Welcome When Staying in Your Home

When I was growing up, my late father had a saying about houseguests: You should treat anyone who comes into your home like a king. If you're not enthusiastic about that idea, guests have no business there, and you shouldn't invite them. Here are ten simple touches to make guests feel welcome and to add elegance to your home.

• Put a fragrant candle, a bowl of potpourri, or a flowering plant in the bedroom and bath to make your home aromatic as well as visually appealing.

• Place a pitcher of ice water and a glass for each guest near the bed.

• Leave a copy of a local city magazine or guidebook on the night table to allow guests to develop their own itinerary and relieve the pressure on you to act as tour guide, entertainment critic, and walking encyclopedia of local trivia.

• Fill a basket or bathroom shelf with aspirin, Band-Aids, toothpaste, a new toothbrush, and other essentials your guests might have forgotten. I also like to collect little soaps, bottles of shampoo, and other hotel toiletries when I travel. Then when guests stay with me, I put all the items in a basket for them to sample and enjoy.

• Empty a few drawers in the dresser your guests will use, clear space in the closet with plenty of matching hangers, and leave room in the bath for guests' toiletries so they won't feel like they're invading your space.

• Remember the basics: Make up the bed with fresh sheets and plenty of pillows. Set out fresh towels and a clean spare robe if you have one.

• Address the house rules. The easiest way to prevent having your household routine destroyed is to leave a note by the guests' bed: "Dear Jim and Sally. We're so glad

A word to the wise: With so many people on fad diets these days, if time permits, I always try to call ahead to find out what my guests will and won't eat. I once invited a friend to lunch who couldn't eat anything I made–not the roasted pepper appetizer, nor the main course of lobster, nor the dessert of fresh raspberries. A quick phone call would have avoided embarrassment for both of us!

Doing the Right Thing: *What do I do if I've planned a dinner party and one guest is more than an hour late?*

If someone arrives late, it's their problem. Don't hold dinner up for the rest of your guests who were considerate enough to show up on time. It will only make you nervous and disrupt everyone else's evening. Remove the place setting and continue without them. Unless the excuse is valid, don't invite them to a seated dinner again; save their invitations for cocktail or buffet parties.

Entertaining His Family and Yours

Inviting the family over can be a great way of getting to know one another. And provided your mother and mother-in-law don't usurp the hostessing duties, it shows both sides of the family that you are independent adults with your own ideas on living.

Since emotions tend to run high at major holidays, it's often good to start small with family entertaining in your new home. You might invite the families over for a Sunday brunch or dinner for no particular occasion. Choosing a "minor" holiday can also be a good way to test family

you're here. Just wanted to let you know a few things about how our house works." Then explain where guests should park their car, whether they should answer the phone or let the machine pick up, and so on. Your guests aren't clairvoyant and would gladly follow a few rules rather than risk offending you.

• In the note explain when you can spend time with your guests and when they will be left on their own. Never feel obligated to overexert yourself and fall behind on your own work; you may end up resenting their visit, and it will show.

• If guests will be on their own often, in your note list favorite lunch and dinner spots, neighborhoods to stroll through, or shows you've enjoyed and how to get tickets.

• Serve a refreshment as soon as your guests arrive, such as a pot of hot tea on a tray in the winter or a pitcher of lemonade in the summer. Prepare these before guests arrive so you won't be frantically squeezing lemons while they're struggling with their suitcases.

How to Be a Considerate Houseguest

Even with the best of intentions, guests irritate their hosts so often that there's an old adage comparing company to fish: After three days both begin to smell. Having spent a good deal of time as both visitor and host, I've developed a simple code of guest etiquette to keep the visit sweet-smelling.

There is no need to buy lavish gifts, heap praise on the hosts' children, or follow a complicated code of conduct. To be a good guest, all you need is a little common sense, courtesy, and sensitivity.

• Always arrive with a gift for the host and hostess. Simple, thoughtful gifts such as a fragrant candle or a basket of wonderful produce from your hometown make a better impression than lavish but generic ones. If you know your hosts' tastes, personalize the gift. If your host enjoys cigars, stop by a local tobacco shop and select a box. For your own sake, choose lightweight gifts; luggage is heavy enough without adding a bottle of Dom Perignon.

• If your hosts have children at home, bring a gift for each child. Again, you needn't spend a lot. A T-shirt, baseball cap, or stuffed animal will show that you are thinking of them as well as their parents. After all, you will be a guest in their home, too.

• During your visit, purchase a special item or two that your hosts wouldn't buy for themselves such as a fine bottle of wine or rare vintage champagne. This is particularly important if the hosts plan to cook for you.

• Neatness counts. Make your bed every morning, and keep the bathroom tidy. Do this even if you don't suspect the hosts will venture into your room or if they have domestic help.

• Replace whatever you use, within reason. If you drink the last of the orange juice or milk, stop by a local grocery to purchase a fresh container.

• Be considerate about use of the telephone. Phone calls

dynamics with minimal stress. For example, host a birthday party for your husband's father or mother, or hold an afternoon tea for both families.

One of the toughest issues for many young married couples is deciding which major holidays you're going to spend with which family. It's a good idea to decide as soon as possible which holidays you'll spend where–at least for this year. Then inform your family of your decision diplomatically but firmly. Your parents might act hurt at first, but they too went through it when they married, and they'll adjust. Painful as it can be, it's an essential step in establishing yourselves as adults.

Many couples agree to alternate holidays, spending Christmas or Chanukah with one side of the family and Thanksgiving with the other. But if you prefer not to miss the holidays with either side of the family, you might consider hosting them yourselves. This can be a fun way to establish new traditions. Let the families contribute by bringing dishes or decorations, but don't let them take over and turn you into a child in your own home. The best way to avoid a "takeover" is to plan the event out carefully and to work together as a couple at hosting. Don't revert back to old behaviors from your single days or childhood, and don't side with your family against your husband. It's important that you and he form a united front. If one family member tends to take charge and dominate family gatherings, either you or your husband could politely remind the person ahead of time that you're hosting and you have specific ideas on what you plan to serve, what time to eat, unwrap gifts, and so on. Sometimes assigning the person a specific task—say, bringing hors d'oeuvres or planning activities to keep the children occupied—can divert their attention so they won't interfere with your plans.

Order some of the dishes rather than trying to prepare an entire holiday banquet yourself; choose easy recipes; and keep lists of everything you'll need to do and buy ahead of time to avoid last-minute panic.

Doing the Right Thing: *If we go out to dinner with our parents, can we offer to pay or will we insult the older generation?*
Generally speaking, if you invited them, you should pay. However, if you're afraid the family will quibble over who gets the bill, discreetly ask the waiter or maître d' ahead of time to bring you the check or give him your credit card beforehand, instructing him to add the gratuity.

If your parents invited you, let them pay. If it was a mutual decision to dine out, you may want to trade off: Let them pay this time, and tell them you'll take care of the bill for the next dinner. Whatever you do, don't make a scene arguing over the bill.

are the source of some of the worst guest faux pas. If you need to make a call, ask for permission. You might also ask whether your hosts have call-waiting and what to do if a call comes in while you are talking. Use a credit card for long-distance calls and limit conversation time to a minimum.

• Leave the room looking as inviting as it was when you arrived. Fold your sheets and towels and put them at the foot of the bed, or ask your hosts where they'd like you to put them. It's unwise to assume you're being helpful by throwing sheets in the washer without asking.

• Avoid getting involved in hosts' disagreements. If you are traveling with a companion, the same concept applies to your relationship: Never argue in front of your hosts or where they might overhear.

• Your visit is not over until you have returned home and sent flowers as well as a sincere thank-you card. If you took pictures during your stay, you might include copies or one framed photograph to remind the hosts of what a wonderful time you spent together. If you've stayed with a family, address your card to the entire family. No matter how busy you are, mail your thank-you within a week of returning home.

Chapter 16

Matters of the Heart

Keeping Romance and Passion Alive

As I have said elsewhere in this book, I've always equated marriages with gardens. If you cultivate a garden, irrigate it, and tend it well, you'll get beautiful flowers to enjoy. The same is true with relationships: If you nurture them, they will blossom. But when you stop caring for your marriage, it will begin to wither away and eventually will go dormant or die.

As newlyweds, most couples are totally in love. Everything seems new and exciting, and your life is filled with passion. You'd never dream that things might not work out. And yet I can't tell you how many couples I've seen divorce after a few years of marriage. "Irreconcilable differences," they claim. Did they try hard enough? Is it possible that they expected the relationship to flourish without bothering to nurture and care for it and without considering that they might have to compromise or make sacrifices? Did they assume passion would keep burning forever without their lifting a finger to stoke the fire? As a woman today, you make an effort to stay in shape, to get ahead in your career, to create a beautiful home. Do not expect something as important as marriage to work automatically without any effort from you.

The Reality of It All

After months of wedding planning, it's tough for some brides to settle into "real life." The honeymoon is over—what now? If you and your husband had different expectations about marriage, petty resentments and disappointments can start to crop up. Romance often wanes as you settle into a routine (what happened to those roses he used to send?), while all his little annoying habits grow more and more noticeable (will he never learn to put the cap back on the toothpaste?).

So what do you do? Start by being realistic. Getting married is the biggest commitment you'll ever make. It says you're prepared to spend the rest of your life with one other human being. Don't focus on what your husband or your marriage will do for you. Realize that marriage is something you and your husband must work on and nurture together. As soon as your wedding has taken place, it's time to start tending the marriage garden.

Sharing Quality Time Together

Always make time for each other, no matter how busy your lives get. I'm not talking about grabbing a bite to eat at the take-out window or flossing your teeth together before bed. Create purposeful, intimate time. Build some ritual into your lives in addition to the impromptu things you do. For example, decide that every Sunday morning you'll have breakfast in bed and later take a leisurely hike together. Or go out on a formal "date" one Saturday night a month. Just as building your career requires planning, structure, and goals, your relationship is your priority and should receive the same attention.

It's important to discover things you can like to do together as a couple. Perhaps you're scuba-diving mates or sports aficionados or history buffs. If so, plan time around those interests: Take a vacation to a great diving destination; get season tickets to see your favorite team; or spend a weekend visiting historic sites in your area.

Learning something new together can be lots of fun. If you both love wine, take a wine-tasting class or go to a good wine shop and buy a selection of bottles to taste together. If you're both music lovers, visit local jazz clubs or plan a weekend trip to a nearby jazz fest. Outdoorsy couples might learn to kayak or take a hike and have a picnic in a park. Another option is to read a new book together and then discuss your thoughts. You can also join local museums for art, natural history, photography, or science and perhaps even meet other couples with similar interests. Or sign up for evening courses in drama, real estate, or whatever else piques your interest at a nearby college. If you use your imagination, the possibilities are endless.

Entertaining as a couple is a wonderful shared activity that has a wealth of benefits. It gives you an opportunity to plan an activity together, to use your favorite things and collect more, and to enjoy your home with your mutual friends.

No matter how much you both adore children, you might consider waiting at least a year or two, getting to really know each other and establishing that you can live up to the marriage commitment, before you bring another human being into the world. The first years of marriage are a very important time for couples in developing a strong, healthy bond as husband and wife.

Once children do enter the picture, intimate time together becomes even more crucial. Quiet weekends away from the children, or at least a night away now and then, are a must to rekindle romance and passion. Why not check into a quaint country inn for a Friday and Saturday night, then have the kids join you on Sunday morning and turn it into a family event? No matter how busy you get with diaper duty or soccer games, it's important to create moments where you can bond as husband and wife, not just Mom and Dad. Pay attention to your intuition; it will tell you when you need to refocus on your relationship.

A word of advice: When you don't share activities or develop common interests, gradually over time you start to live separate lives. The more separate your lives become, the fewer opportunities you'll have to work together, laugh, and enjoy each other's company.

Healthy Time Apart

On the other hand, spending every waking hour with your husband is probably not such a good idea.

Time apart is important for husbands and wives. It's part of what makes you interesting. Don't fall into the old cliché of trying to become one with your spouse. I've seen this happen many times. All too suddenly couples start to talk alike, dress alike, even think alike. It's inevitable that you'll develop some similarities because you spend so much time together, but always maintain your own interests, hobbies, and opinions. Be yourself. Remember what drew him to you in the first place.

In addition to your life as a married couple, you both have individual lives that deserve respect. In the most successful marriages, the husband and wife have activities that they enjoy on their own as well as those they share.

Personal space can be a sticking point, especially if you've lived alone. If you're going to spend the rest of your lives together, you'll have to get used to sharing. But be respectful of each other's privacy. When I was growing up, neither my father nor any of us children would ever have dared look in my mother's purse. It was private. The same is true of his briefcase, your mail, or whatever else the two of you consider private.

Speaking of privacy, never discuss personal things about your husband with outsiders, no matter if you're mad at him or if your friends are sharing the juiciest details of their sex lives. Before revealing anything about your relationship to others, ask yourself:

Would he really want others to know what I'm about to tell?

How would he feel if he knew I was sharing it?

Would I want him telling this to anyone else about me?

If the answer is no, don't go there.

Trust, Flirtation, and the Green-Eyed Monster

To me, the three things that count most in life are sincerity, honesty, and integrity. With these you have trust, which is the foundation for a happy, successful marriage. All good relationships are based on trust; without it you have nothing.

When trust is the foundation of a relationship, there is never a reason for jealousy or possessiveness. For husbands and wives in good marriages, it's healthy to have fantasies about other people now and then, to look at other people you find attractive, and even to flirt as long as you know when to come back to home base and appreciate what is yours. I really believe that that makes for a more successful relationship than repressing your fantasies. A little harmless flirtation can boost your self-esteem and reaffirm your attractiveness to the opposite sex. Note that flirting is completely different from having an intent to take things to the next level. Just make sure you understand the difference and don't violate your husband's trust. By the way, just because you're married, there's no reason to stop flirting with your husband.

When you start a marriage, it's like a piece of fine crystal. It's flawless. If you break that glass by

Ten Ideas to Keep the Fire Burning

Marriage and family therapists Dr. Leslie Pam and his wife, Ann Christie, M.A., both very dear friends of mine, have been helping couples find solutions to their problems and develop stronger, healthier relationships for many years. Not only that, but Leslie and Ann practice what they preach. Theirs is one of the happiest marriages I know. Following are Leslie and Ann's guidelines to help ensure that your life together is a long, loving, and fulfilling one.

• Do something loving and thoughtful for your partner every single day. Never ask "What's he done for me lately?" Ask "What can I do to make him happy today?" Positive thoughts and feelings generate goodwill and happiness for both of you.

• Create great memories together. They'll help you through the rough times.

• Be honest with yourself and with him. Don't expect him to pick up on all your subtle cues and moods, just tell him what you're thinking. And be open to his thoughts and observations. Never be defensive.

• Take responsibility for your own sexual fulfillment. He's not a mind reader. The best way to get what you want is to tell him—or show him. Likewise, be open-minded and receptive when he tells you what he wants.

• Understand the differences between men and women. Their language, communication styles, sexual needs, and many other areas are quite disparate. Don't expect him to think like you or respond as you would. Let him be himself.

• Embrace the positive and inevitable changes in your relationship. Stop struggling with things that don't work. All marriages evolve, and that change paves the way for new growth and vitality.

• Learn to be a good listener, and teach him how. Men tend to be solution-oriented, so remind him that you're not asking him to solve your problems, you just want him to listen.

breaching the trust you've created, no matter what glue you use, there will always be a crack or a bit of residue. So before you ever consider venturing out of the boundaries of trust, realize that you're going to destroy something very precious.

The Element of Surprise

Never allow yourself to fall into a rut. When you get bored, your eyes start to wander—and so will his. Always appeal to the unexpected. As long as you're unpredictable, you're exciting.

There's nothing wrong with answering the door in a sheer negligee and heels with a fabulous bottle of champagne, or e-mailing your husband an invitation for a romantic date and a candlelit bubble bath or a fantasy evening. When it comes to Valentine's Day and your anniversary, perhaps you can agree that one of you will orchestrate one year and the other the next. That way you're both contributing to keeping the element of surprise in your romance.

So many couples forget how exciting and easy it is to build surprise into their everyday lives. Perhaps your husband used to show up with flowers on a whim when you were dating, but now he buys them so infrequently that the first thing you think when you see roses is, "What's he done wrong?" Or maybe you used to hide lacy lingerie under your most conservative suit as a surprise for your husband, but now you toss on an old T-shirt and sweatpants for bed every night.

Why limit sending flowers and buying gifts to holidays? The best time to give someone a present is for no reason at all. Write a love note, pick up a new CD he's been wanting or an old one with a song you heard on your first date, or bake his favorite dessert. You don't need to be extravagant; it's the little unexpected, thoughtful gestures that count. They send a message that even when he's not with you, you are thinking of him fondly.

Never Let Yourself Go–Constant Maintenance

For your own self-respect and for the sake of the marriage, both husband and wife should keep in mind what attracted you to each other initially, and maintain it. So what if you can't be a perfect size four for the rest of your life? Both of you can always make sure that you look attractive, you can watch what you eat, and you can keep yourselves in shape. If the attraction was there in the beginning between you and your husband, then it can be there forever.

If you both sense that you are starting to let yourselves go, try to find a nice way to tell each other. Don't point out love handles while your spouse is putting a cream puff in his mouth at dessert. Instead, encourage each other to get back into a sport you enjoy, try a new hairstyle, join a gym together–whatever you think might help. Remember, these suggestions are made because you both want to feel good about yourselves, not because you disapprove of each other.

Let's Talk About Sex

First, the good news: Don't worry. Chances are pretty good that your wedding night wasn't the best sex you'll ever have. If you had sex at all after such an exhilarating and exhausting day, you've done better than most newlyweds! Most

• Make important decisions in your lives only when you're in agreement. Deciding you're ready to have a baby and then surprising your husband by showing him the result of a home pregnancy test, or driving home in a new sports car you bought with the money slotted for a house is a recipe for disaster. Communicate and cooperate, especially on major issues.

• Live your dreams, and let him live his. If he loves luxury cruises and you love roughing it with a backpack and a compass, alternate choosing vacations. Play tennis with him one Sunday, and convince him to shop with you the next. It's very important to trade off likes and dislikes and to be a good sport about it. If you make the mistake of limiting your hobbies, cuisine, music, sports, and other activities to those you share, you'll shut yourselves off from so much. Be open to new experiences, and indulge your partner in the things he loves.

• Have faith in your husband, your marriage, and your future. Why waste time plagued by doubts or fears? Expect the best. That's the surest way to make it happen.

Aphrodisiacs: Foods of Love

For centuries, everyone from poets to scientists has acknowledged a link between food and love. Scientists say it's because chocolate, almonds, avocados, and certain other foods are full of an amino acid that gives us an endorphin rush, not unlike sex. Poets claim the rounded, sensual shape of a peach simply awakens our animal instincts. Whichever explanation you prefer, here are fifteen of the all-time top aphrodisiacs from the kitchen.

Bananas

Black olives

Caviar

Champagne

Chocolate

Grapes

Honey

Ice cream

Lobster

Oysters

Peaches

Pomegranates

Raspberries

Strawberries

Whipped cream

married couples, women especially, say the best is yet to come in the bedroom. Sex actually gets better as you break down inhibitions and boundaries and become more relaxed and comfortable with each other.

Now the bad news: It won't happen automatically. Like everything else worth having, you've got to give some thought to sex to keep it exciting.

Start by being honest. Tell him–or, better yet, show him–what you like and dislike, what you would like to try, and what makes you uncomfortable. Spend some time figuring out your turn-ons and turn-offs.

And no faking it. Experts estimate that as many as 90 percent of women have faked an orgasm at some point in their lives. Well, now's the time to stop. Trust is the key to a successful, happy marriage. How would you feel if you found out he'd been faking it all this time because he didn't want to hurt your feelings?

Remember that the surprise factor works for sex as well as marriage. Schedule a romantic date, and wear a seductive new outfit. Read erotic literature aloud together; find a new place to make love; take him to a sex shop and find something that you two might both like to experiment with–do whatever you think sounds exciting. Chances are if you're turned on, he will be, too.

Don't overlook nonsexual intimacy. Simply giving your husband a back rub or lying in bed in the dark listening to him talk can be not only sensual but an excellent way to reestablish intimacy.

Of course, sex isn't the final word on whether you'll have a good life together, but it is certainly a good litmus test. I know so many people who say, "We haven't had sex in four years. She's my best friend." If that's the case, someone is going to start shopping around soon. If you're not having sex, a red flag should go up immediately. Start to explore the reasons you're abstaining and how to get back on track. It might have nothing to do with your relationship. Perhaps work is exhausting you both. Maybe you're tense about the holidays. Sex is often the first thing to go. As soon as you identify the problem, you can start to remedy it and ensure that it doesn't cause a rift in your marriage. If a steamy weekend getaway might clear your head and help you bond with your husband, take it no matter how busy you are. After all, it's what you're working for anyway. Never assume you'll be able to pick up where you left off after tax season, after the holidays, or after you finish the last big project at the office. Hurt feelings and resentment may build up and your spouse may feel he's less important than everyone else in your life. Keep your priorities straight. You can always get another job, but your spouse is irreplaceable.

Chapter 17

Disagreements

How to Survive and Resolve Them

I f you've planned a wedding, you're probably well past your first argument. Some brides get enough practice in the art of negotiation and compromise during the planning of their wedding that they're practically ready for a life in politics! Even if you and your husband are the world's most easygoing couple, you're bound to run up against a disagreement sooner or later. Developing an arsenal of positive–rather than destructive–negotiating tactics will help protect your marriage through the rough times. Following is a blueprint to get you started.

• Never try to win. When it comes to resolving an argument, don't focus on who's right and who's wrong; focus on how can you move forward and make sure it won't happen again. We all argue, and no one is entirely right. Never persecute him for a mistake. Your mission is not to make him feel guilty or to prove that you'd make the better trial lawyer. Your only goals should be to improve your relationship, to grow closer, and to find a way to be more considerate of each other. Always acknowledge your part in the conflict and remember, the best outcome is always a compromise.

• Ban cruel and unusual argument tactics. We've all been in scenarios where we're not talking to each other, and we all know the silent treatment doesn't work. Set ground rules for arguing: no silent treatment. No harboring grudges and unloading twenty complaints that have been building up over the past six months. Resolve to discuss a problem as soon as you're aware of it, and focus on only one at a time. If you've developed hurtful, negative habits, getting rid of them will create room for change and growth.

• Cool down. Never argue in the heat of the moment. It's like pouring gasoline on a fire. You'll both say nasty things that will hurt each other and that you'll regret. Instead, take some time to think about what happened, and let the emotion dissipate. Discuss problems only when you're thinking logically and clearly. In my personal and business life, I never confront anyone when I'm seething. That negative energy is like an infection; it affects everyone and everything. Always wait until you have calmed down. Then instead of a screaming match, you can have an amicable discussion and find out how to make things work better in the future rather than harping on what didn't work before.

• If anger is a problem for you, find a constructive outlet to vent it. Take a walk, hit the gym, go to a movie by yourself. Try to figure out what's underneath the problem: Are you feeling threatened? Hurt? Disappointed? If it helps you organize your thoughts, write down what you feel and what you'd like to accomplish or resolve. You might even find the answers come from within. Perhaps you're ticked off at your husband because he's not supportive when you discuss your problems at the office. When you explore your real feelings, you might decide that you need to assert yourself at work or make a career change. (It's easy to let problems at work monopolize your conversations and put a damper on your relationship. If you sense this happening, set a time limit of a half hour or less for each of you to discuss work in the evening. Ban shop talk for the rest of the night or weekend.)

• If you must have a disagreement, pick your time with care. Never get into a fight when you're about to have dinner with friends. You'll both feel awkward, and your friends will sense something's wrong. Don't bring up a problem when he's just brought home flowers, on his birthday, or when he's taking you to dinner or making another affectionate gesture.

• Watch your language. Avoid attack-mode phrases like "You never take out the trash" or "You always ignore me when you're with your friends." Instead say, "It's important to me that we share household chores" or "I feel like I'm not a part of the conversation when we're out with your friends." These are nonthreatening phrases, and they leave room for him to find solutions rather than defend himself. Don't rant; let him get a word in edgewise, too. Your goal is to communicate, not pontificate. Once you've cooled down, find a nonaccusatory way to bring up the subject for discussion. For example, "You know, I'd like to discuss something with you. I love you madly, but something happened the other evening that really upset me, and I want to talk it over so that we can avoid it in the future."

Body language counts. Try not to tense up, turn away from him when he's talking, fold your arms across your chest, or–even worse–shake your finger at him. Keep your arms and shoulders relaxed. (Crossed arms, hands, or legs send the message "keep away" or "back off.") Face him and use frequent eye contact, possibly a reassuring touch now and then.

Never swallow your anger. Women often "go along to get along." They hold their tongue rather than express their feelings because they don't want to ruin an enjoyable Saturday night, or they worry that they're overreacting, or they just hate to fight. Never compromise yourself; it turns you into a victim, and there's no place for victims in healthy relationships. Your anger will come out one way or another, whether you pout, cry, or become passive-aggressive and forget his birthday. While you certainly should never yell, it's essential to find an effective way to cope with your feelings. Research indicates that repressed rage is one of the primary reasons that heart attacks are on the rise among women. Finding a healthy outlet for your anger can protect your health as well as your marriage.

If you don't feel you have the ability to take these steps on your own, visit a family therapist or marriage counselor. Never avoid seeking professional help just because it's your first year of marriage and "things will get better." Asking for help doesn't mean you're failing; it means you care enough to take action to protect your relationship. If your dog is ill, you go to the veterinarian. If you've got a fever, you go to the doctor. Your marriage is the thing you cherish most in your life, and if you need help to keep it on track, don't hesitate. The longer you pretend that nothing's wrong, the deeper the roots of your problems grow.

I have always believed that things happen to teach us a lesson. There are no negative circumstances; the only negative is us complaining that "things didn't go our own way." In other words, our own selfish ego gets in the way. If each situation teaches us a lesson, then what we thought was negative becomes positive. If we don't learn from these situations, they will come back to haunt us again and again. Each time the pain will be sharper and the hurdles will be higher, until we're finally forced to deal with reality and face the truth about why this happened to us in the first place. Unfortunately, sometimes we've wasted too much time by then, and it's too late to save the relationship.

Most marital problems crop up when our lives get out of control—when we allow career, family, friends, hobbies, or obsessions to creep in and take precedence over our relationships. Suddenly we're being considerate of everyone but the person we love the most. Why? Because we think we can get away with it. "You're my lover, I thought you would understand." That's absolutely the worst thing you can do. Your spouse is the most sacred person in your life. No matter what external stresses arise, you should work to form a united front against the world. Love means laughing at the same old jokes and stories you've heard a hundred times; it means supporting each other through the good times and the bad ones, and it means always treating each other with respect. Lose your temper with an acquaintance or a professional associate if you must, but never at the person you love. And always stay alert to what's happening in your life—problems at work, pressure from your parents or kids, financial troubles, or anything else that could affect your marriage.

Of course, every relationship will have ups and downs. But if you treat the downs well, the ups become so much better. To me, marriages are like oscilloscopes. You'll have moments when you're farther apart and moments when you feel totally connected. When you're first married, those margins are higher. Then as you settle in, the highs and lows become less extreme. True, some of the drama might wear off, but the times you're operating on the same wavelength become more frequent and longer-lasting.

Finally, keep in mind that no matter what problems you encounter, they can always be sorted out. It just depends on when you pick your moment, what tone of voice you choose, and whether you're willing to compromise. And after all, life is all about compromise.

A Few Final Thoughts

Celebrating Married Life to Its Fullest

I have always believed that the laws of life are extremely simple. The more you put into anything in life, the greater benefits and enjoyment you will reap. It's no different from the way you would treat a plant. The more you nourish it, the sweeter the fruit or the more beautiful the bloom. The same principle applies not only to your marriage, but to everything you do. It's like elementary physics: What you get out is what you put in.

In all avenues of life, I have always believed in going the extra mile. The more care with which we treat people, the more we are loved and respected by those around us. Although we live in an age of nanoseconds, sound bites, and New York minutes, and there is so much pressure to rush through our days, I hope this book will encourage you to slow down and take a few extra moments or a few extra steps to go the extra mile and add more graciousness and meaning to your daily life and your relationships. That is all it takes to be considerate of others and to live a much more rewarding life.

Some of the happiest moments of my life have been spent surrounded by fabulous friends and caring family, laughing and telling stories at an impromptu candlelit dinner, enjoying wine and delicious food. I hope this book has inspired you to create those magical moments and to enjoy your wedding as well as your marriage to its fullest. During the months that you and your fiancé spend designing a unique and personal celebration, the wedding day itself, and the first years of marriage, you will discover new dimensions and add potential to your relationship. All of these are once-in-a-lifetime experiences. Make the most of them.

The most important aspect of life is our own attitude. I believe that we live in an all-positive world. There is no such thing as negative. The "negative" things that are placed before us are the lessons we need to learn in order to elevate ourselves. If we learn from them, then they are no longer negative; they are positive. If you embrace this attitude in your life, you will live an existence filled with appreciation, grace, and humility. These are the qualities that will pave the way for an eternally happy marriage and will allow you to instill the right principles in your children.

My sincerest congratulations and very best wishes for a fabulous wedding and a wonderful life together filled with much fun, good health, love, peace, prosperity, travel, excitement, joy, friendship, and abundant happiness.

Colin

A Calendar and Checklist

Six to Twelve Months Before the Wedding

Make decisions about the style of wedding you want.

Set a tentative date and time for the wedding, pending confirmation that the location you want is available.

Determine the budget.

Research locations and book the space.

Retain the officiant for the ceremony.

Decide how many guests you will invite, and begin developing the guest list.

Research wedding vendors, such as florist, caterer, photographer, cake baker, and band.

Ask your maid or matron of honor, bridesmaids, and other attendants (if you have them) to serve, and inform them of all pertinent dates.

Interview photographers and videographers.

Work with your fiancé in selecting your registry items.

When the date, time of day, location, style, and level of formality of your wedding have been determined, shop for wedding dress, shoes, and accessories.

Select bridesmaids' attire.

Consult with your groom on the men's wedding attire.

Three to Six Months Before the Wedding

Check the requirements for blood tests, physical exams, and the marriage license in the state where you will be married.

Shop for wedding rings, allowing time to have them engraved if desired.

Begin planning the honeymoon. Popular destinations during high season may need to be booked three to six months in advance (or more).

Finalize the guest list.

Have invitations (and personal stationery, if desired) designed and printed.

Make final selection of wedding vendors, and sign contracts. Note that vendors who are very much in demand may have to be booked up to a year in advance.

Plan the type of rehearsal dinner you will have, and book the space.

Reserve blocks of rooms, if necessary, for out-of-town wedding guests.

Book wedding night accommodations, if different from honeymoon accommodations.

Hire wedding-related transportation (vans, limousines), if necessary.

Discuss and finalize attendants' duties.

Make honeymoon air travel, ground transportation, and hotel arrangements.

Two to Three Months Before the Wedding

Finalize details with wedding vendors.

Finalize details of ceremony with officiant.

Finalize rehearsal dinner details.

Book massage professional for morning of wedding day.

Book wedding-related grooming professionals (facialist, manicurist) as needed.

Have blood test and physical exam.

Purchase wedding party gifts.

Four to Six Weeks Before the Wedding

Mail wedding invitations.

Mail rehearsal dinner invitations, if sent separately.

Begin writing thank-you notes with groom for wedding presents.

Compose, design, and print ceremony program, if necessary.

Confirm all wedding vendor contracts and deposits.

Have final fittings of your wedding dress and attendants' dresses.

Have reception menu tasting along with sample table setting and centerpiece by florist.

Make changes to banking information, insurance policies, wills, and other legal documents.

Prepare wedding announcements for newspapers and/or magazines, if desired. Save to send with wedding photo after ceremony.

Select wedding gift for groom.

Confirm date and time of wedding rehearsal with officiant and entire wedding party.

Two Weeks Before the Wedding

Double-check and reconfirm all wedding-related arrangements.

Call guests who failed to respond to the wedding invitation to find out if they are attending.

Plan and finalize seating assignments at reception.

Get haircut.

Have a facial.

Have teeth cleaned by oral hygienist.

Visit salon for trial run of wedding-day makeup and hairstyle (with headpiece, if you will be wearing one), making sure you see the effect in the same lighting that will prevail at your ceremony and reception. Take a photograph for the makeup artist and hairstylist to use as a reference for the wedding day. Also note the amount of time required for hair and makeup, and reserve extra time on your wedding day.

If you will be sending out wedding announcements, address, seal, and stamp them.

Obtain marriage license with fiancé.

Pick up wedding rings from jeweler.

Double-check and reconfirm all honeymoon travel arrangements.

During the Week Before the Wedding

Give final guest count to caterer or hotel.

Pack for the honeymoon.

Arrange for someone to mail your wedding announcements on the wedding day.

Assemble all elements of your wedding attire.

The day before or the day of the wedding, have a manicure and pedicure.

Make sure you, your parents, and/or your groom have in hand all wedding gratuities and checks for balances due to vendors.

Confirm all honeymoon arrangements.

Attend the wedding rehearsal with your groom and wedding party.

Attend the rehearsal dinner, and get to bed early the night before the wedding!

The Wedding Day

Have a relaxing massage.

Have hair styled and makeup applied.

Dress with help of mother, attendants.

Have wedding gift and note delivered to groom.

Arrive at ceremony site on time.

Focus on your groom's enjoyment while having a great time yourself!

After the Wedding

While on your honeymoon, write to your parents to thank them. A gift of flowers delivered to their home is a lovely gesture.

Write thank-you notes promptly.

Acknowledgments

Because of the ever-changing trends that affect the plan and design of weddings, there is always a need for another bridal book. I am forever grateful to all the brides from whom I have learned so much and who have offered me so much inspiration.

The part I enjoyed most about the creation of this book was the opportunity to work with many talented people. To all these go my thanks: including the Bantam Dell Publishing Group, especially editors Kathleen Jayes and Diane Bartoli, my agent, Margret McBride at the McBride Literary Agency. A big thank-you to Jean Barrett, who helped me write this book, and to my partner, Stuart Brownstein, whose knowledge has also been imparted in its pages.

I would also like to thank my dedicated and talented staff in Los Angeles and New York who does so much to make our weddings elegant and memorable. And special thanks to my partner in Los Angeles, David Berke.

Thanks to all the talented photographers who captured the magical moments that appear in this book: Deborah Feingold, Joe Buissink, Stephanie Jasper and Paul Sky from Jasper Sky, Magnus Lanje, Alison Duke, Beth Herzhaft, and Scott Streble.

A huge thanks to Sam Shahid, Carlos Frederico Farina, and Kelly Olsen from Shahid & Company for the tasteful and exquisite book design.

I am forever grateful to my parents who instilled in me the importance of being a gentleman. Their teachings have guided me over the years and have allowed me to create a style of my own.

FOR THE BRIDE

Published by Delacorte Press, Random House, Inc.

1540 Broadway, New York, New York, 10036

Delacorte Press® is a registered trademark of Random House, Inc.,
and the colophon is a trademark of Random House, Inc.

Library of Congress Cataloging-in-Publication Data is on file with the publisher

ISBN: 0-385-33442-7

Book design by Shahid & Company

Manufactured in the United States of America.
Published simultaneously in Canada.

January 2000

10 9 8 7 6 5 4 3 2

RRD

www.ColinCowie.com